KB043835

Reading Schedule

이 책은 총 17,000여개의 단어로 구성되어 있습니다.(중복 포함, 1페이지는 대략 70단어)
분당 150단어 읽기는 원어민이 말하는 속도입니다. 먼저 이 기준을 목표로 시작해보세요.

● 1회 읽기

날 짜	/	/	/	/	/
시 간	~	~	~	~	~
페이지	~	~	~	~	~

내용 이해도 ✓ 90%이상 ✓ 70% ✓ 50% ✓ 30%이하

리딩속도 계산 [244] ÷ [   ] × [70] = [   ]

전체 페이지   시간(분)   1페이지 당 평균 단어수   분당 읽은 단어수

● 2회 읽기

날 짜	/	/	/	/	/
시 간	~	~	~	~	~
페이지	~	~	~	~	~

내용 이해도 ✓ 90%이상 ✓ 70% ✓ 50% ✓ 30%이하

리딩속도 계산 [244] ÷ [   ] × [70] = [   ]

전체 페이지   시간(분)   1페이지 당 평균 단어수   분당 읽은 단어수

● 3회 읽기

날 짜	/	/	/	/	/
시 간	~	~	~	~	~
페이지	~	~	~	~	~

내용 이해도 ✓ 90%이상 ✓ 70% ✓ 50% ✓ 30%이하

리딩속두 계산 [244] ÷ [   ] × [70] = [   ]

전체 페이지   시간(분)   1페이지 당 평균 단어수   분당 읽은 단어수

식은 죽
먹기야~

● 전체 평가

체감 난이도 ☑ 상 ☑ 상중 ☑ 중 ☑ 중하 ☑ 하

읽기 만족도 ☑ 나는 리딩의 고수!

☑ 좀 잘했군요~

☑ 노력하세요.

☑ 난 머리가 안 좋나봐 -.-;

이솝 우화

리딩 속도가 빨라지는 영어책 013

이솝 우화
AESOP'S FABLES

2020년 10월 10일 초판 1쇄 인쇄
2020년 10월 15일 초판 1쇄 발행

지은이 이솝
발행인 손건
편집기획 김상배
마케팅 이언영
디자인 이성세
제작 최승용
인쇄 선경프린테크

발행처 LanCom 랜컴
주소 서울시 금천구 시흥대로193, 709호
등록번호 제 312-2006-00060호
전화 02) 2636-0895
팩스 02) 2636-0896
홈페이지 www.lancom.co.kr

ISBN 979-11-89204-70-9 13740

이솝 우화

AESOP'S FABLES

이솝 지음

LanCom
Language & Communication

CONTENTS

THE FOX AND THE GRAPES

A hungry Fox saw some fine bunches of
배고픈, 굶주리는 여우   질 높은   다발, 송이, 묶음
Grapes hanging from a vine that was
포도   …에 걸린[매달린/드리워진]   포도나무(덩굴)
trained along a high trellis, and did his best to
…를 따라 가꾸어진   (덩굴나무가 타고 올라가도록 만든) 격자 구조물
reach them by jumping as high as he could into
…에 이르다[닿다/도달하다]   할 수 있는 한 높이   공중으로
the air. But it was all in vain, for they were just
                        허사가 되어, 보람도 없이, 부질없이, 괜히
out of reach: so he gave up trying, and walked
                    give up: 포기하다   떠나버리다(walk away)
away with an air of dignity and unconcern,
       점잔빼며, 자신만만하게   위엄, 품위; 자존감   무심, 무관심
remarking, "I thought those Grapes were ripe,
언급[말/논평/발언]하다   익은, 숙성한
but I see now they are quite sour."
                        꽤, 상당히 (맛이) 신, 시큼한

THE GOOSE THAT LAID THE GOLDEN EGGS

A Man and his Wife had the good fortune to
다행히도[운 좋게도] ···하다
possess a Goose which laid a Golden Egg
소유[소지/보유]하다   거위   (알을) 낳다(lay)
every day. Lucky though they were, they soon
운이 좋은, 행운의   ···이긴 하지만[···인데도]
began to think they were not getting rich fast
시작하다   생각하다   get rich: 부자가 되다
enough, and, imagining the bird must be made
필요한 만큼의[충분한]   상상하다   (마음속으로) 그리다
of gold inside, they decided to kill it in order to
···의 안[속/내부]에   결심하다   죽이다   ~하기 위해[~하려고]
secure the whole store of precious metal at once.
얻어 내다, 획득[확보]하다 저장[보관]하다 귀금속   즉시; 한꺼번에
But when they cut it open they found it was just
베다, 자르다, 절개하다   찾다(find)
like any other goose. Thus, they neither got rich
같은, 동일한(equal)   (둘 중) 어느 것도 ···아니다
all at once, as they had hoped, nor enjoyed any
                    have hope: 희망을 가지다   누리다, 향유하다
longer the daily addition to their wealth.
           나날의   추가, 부가   부(富), (많은) 재산

Much wants more and loses all.
원하다, 바라다   잃어버리다, 분실하다

THE MISCHIEVOUS DOG

There was once a Dog who used to snap at
…하곤 했다   …에 달려들다
people and bite them without any provoca-
        (이빨로) 물다   도발, 자극; 화낼 이유
tion, and who was a great nuisance to every one
                              귀찮은 사람[것/일], 골칫거리
who came to his master's house. So his master
                          주인
fastened a bell round his neck to warn people of
매다, 채우다   목   경고하다, 주의를 주다
his presence.
    (특정한 곳에) 있음, 존재(함), 참석

The Dog was very proud of the bell, and
                      …을 자랑으로 여기다, 의기 양양해 하다
strutted about tinkling it with immense satisfac-
뽐내며 걷다   딸랑딸랑 (울리는)   엄청난, 어마어마한   만족(감)
tion. But an old dog came up to him and said,
"The fewer airs you give yourself the better, my
    (수가) 약간의[여러/몇](복수 명사동사와 함께 쓰임)
friend. You don't think, do you, that your bell
                        생각하다
was given you as a reward of merit? On the con-
                        보상   훌륭한 요소, 장점   그와는 반대로
trary, it is a badge of disgrace."
                  표, 배지   망신, 수치, 불명예 (=shame)

Notoriety is often mistaken for fame.
악명, 악평   자주, 흔히, 보통   오해[오인]하다   명성

18

THE MICE IN COUNCIL

Once upon a time all the Mice met together in Council, and discussed the best means of securing themselves against the attacks of the cat. After several suggestions had been debated, a Mouse of some standing and experience got up and said, "I think I have hit upon a plan which will ensure our safety in the future, provided you approve and carry it out. It is that we should fasten a bell round the neck of our enemy the cat, which will by its tinkling warn us of her approach."

This proposal was warmly applauded, and it had been already decided to adopt it, when an old Mouse got upon his feet and said, "I agree with you all that the plan before us is an admirable one: but may I ask who is going to bell the cat?"

THE DOG AND THE SOW

A Dog and a Sow were arguing and each claimed that its own young ones were finer than those of any other animal.

"Well," said the Sow at last, "mine can see, at any rate, when they come into the world: but yours are born blind."

THE SPENDTHRIFT AND THE SWALLOW

A Spendthrift, who had wasted his fortune,
돈을 헤프게 쓰는 사람   낭비하다   재산, 부; 거금
and had nothing left but the clothes in
~말고는 아무 것도 남아 있지 않다   옷, 의복
which he stood, saw a Swallow one fine day in
제비   날씨가 좋은 날
early spring.
이른 봄

Thinking that summer had come, and that
여름
he could now do without his coat, he went and

sold it for what it would fetch.
(돈을 받고) 팔다(sell)   (특정 가격에) 팔리다

A change, however, took place in the
변화   어쨌든, 하지만
weather, and there came a sharp frost which
날씨   된서리
killed the unfortunate Swallow.
운이 없는[나쁜], 불운한

When the Spendthrift saw its dead body he
시체
cried, "Miserable bird! Thanks to you I am per-
비참한, 불쌍한   ~덕분에   얼어 죽을 것 같은
ishing of cold myself."

One swallow does not make summer.
제비   여름

THE FOX AND THE CROW

A Crow was sitting on a branch of a tree with
a piece of cheese in her beak when a Fox
observed her and set his wits to work to discover
some way of getting the cheese.
Coming and standing under the tree he
looked up and said, "What a noble bird I see
above me! Her beauty is without equal, the hue
of her plumage exquisite. If only her voice is as
sweet as her looks are fair, she ought without
doubt to be Queen of the Birds."
The Crow was hugely flattered by this, and
just to show the Fox that she could sing she gave
a loud caw. Down came the cheese, of course,
and the Fox, snatching it up, said, "You have a
voice, madam, I see: what you want is wits."

THE OLD WOMAN AND THE DOCTOR

An Old Woman became almost totally
거의(=nearly)   완전히 눈이 먼
blind from a disease of the eyes, and,
질병   눈
after consulting a Doctor, made an agreement
자문, 조언; 진찰   의사   동의, 협정, 합의, 승낙
with him in the presence of witnesses that she
참석, 존재(함)   목격자, 증인
should pay him a high fee if he cured her, while
지불하다   높은 수수료   낫게 하다, (병을) 치유하다
if he failed he was to receive nothing.
실패하다, …하지 못하다   받다, 받아들이다
The Doctor accordingly prescribed a course
그런 이유로, 그래서   처방을 내리다, 처방하다   과정
of treatment, and every time he paid her a visit
치료, 처치   pay ~ a visit ~를 방문하다
he took away with him some article out of the
가져가다   물품[물건] (=item)
house, until at last, when he visited her for the
~까지   마침내, 결국   방문하다
last time, and the cure was complete, there was
치료, 치유   완료하다, 끝마치다
nothing left.

When the Old Woman saw that the house
was empty she refused to pay him his fee; and,
비어 있는, 빈   거절하다   지불하다   요금, 수수료
after repeated refusals on her part, he sued her
반복[되풀이]하다   거절, 거부   고소하다, 소송을 제기하다
before the magistrates for payment of her debt.
치안 판사   지불, 지급, 납입   빚, 부채
On being brought into court she was ready with
법정, 법원   ~할 준비가 되다
her.

"The claimant," said she, "has stated the
(권리의) 청구인   정해진, 정기의
facts about our agreement correctly. I undertook
(입증할 수 있는) 사실   바르게, 정확하게   약속하다, 동의하다
to pay him a fee if he cured me, and he, on his
part, promised to charge nothing if he failed.
약속하다   (~에 대한) 요금
Now, he says I am cured; but I say that I am
말하다
blinder than ever, and I can prove what I say.
눈이 더 먼   입증하다, 증명하다
When my eyes were bad I could at any rate
나쁜, 형편없는   어쨌든, 적어도
see well enough to be aware that my house
필요한 만큼의, 충분한   ···을 알아 차리다, ···을 알다
contained a certain amount of furniture and
···이 들어[함유되어] 있다   일정량의, 많은 양의 ~ 가구
other things; but now, when according to him I
~에 따라
am cured, I am entirely unable to see anything
치료하다, 치유하다   전적으로, 완전히, 전부
there at all."
전혀

THE CAT AND THE BIRDS

A Cat heard that the Birds in an aviary were
ailing. So he got himself up as a doctor,
and, taking with him a set of the instruments
proper to his profession, presented himself at
the door, and inquired after the health of the
Birds.

"We shall do very well," they replied, without
letting him in, "when we've seen the last of you."

A villain may disguise himself, but he will
not deceive the wise.

THE ASS, THE FOX, AND THE LION

An Ass and a Fox went into partnership
당나귀   여우   (사업의) 동업자임
and sallied out to forage for food to-
      힘차게 떠나다   먹이를 찾다
gether.

They hadn't gone far before they saw a Lion
              멀리 가다   사자
coming their way, at which they were both
                                          둘 다
dreadfully frightened.
몹시, 굉장히   겁먹은, 무서워하는

But the Fox thought he saw a way of saving
                    생각하다   ~하는 방법
his own skin, and went boldly up to the Lion
                              대담하게
and whispered in his ear, "I'll manage that you
        속삭이다   귀에 대고   (힘든 일을) 간신히[용케] 해내다
shall get hold of the Ass without the trouble of
    ~을 붙잡다   문제, 곤란, 골칫거리
stalking him, if you'll promise to let me go free."
  ~을 따라다니며 괴롭히기, 스토킹   약속하다   놓아주다

The Lion agreed to this, and the Fox then
              동의하다, 승낙하다
rejoined his companion and contrived before
다시 합류하다   동반자, 동행   용케[어떻게든] …하다
long to lead him by a hidden pit, which some
        안내하다, 이끌다   숨겨진   구덩이
hunter had dug as a trap for wild animals, and
사냥꾼   (구멍 등을) 파다 함정, 덫   야수, 들짐승, 야생동물
into which he fell.

28

When the Lion saw that the Ass was safely
안전하게
caught and couldn't get away, it was to the

Fox that he first turned his attention, and he
주의 (집중),주목; 관심, 흥미
soon finished him off, and then at his leisure
곧   ~을 죽이다[없애 버리다]   한가하게, 느긋하게
proceeded to feast upon the Ass.
계속해서…을 하다   맘껏 먹다[포식하다]

Betray a friend, and you'll often find you
배신[배반]하다   자주; 흔히, 보통
have ruined yourself.
망치다, 파멸하다

THE MOON AND HER MOTHER

The Moon once begged her Mother to make
달   애원하다, 간청하다   어머니
her a gown.
특별한 경우에 입는 여성의) 드레스

"How can I?" replied she; "there's no fitting
…에 꼭 맞다
your figure. At one time you're a New Moon,
모습, 몸매   초승달
and at another you're a Full Moon; and between
보름달   ~사이[중간]에
whiles you're neither one nor the other."

THE BOYS AND THE FROGS

Some mischievous Boys were playing on the
짓궂은, 말썽꾸러기의
edge of a pond, and, catching sight of some
~의 끝, 가장자리   연못
Frogs swimming about in the shallow water,
개구리   수영하는   얕은
they began to amuse themselves by pelting them
            즐겁게[미소 짓게/재미있게] 하다   (무엇을 던지며) 공격하다
with stones, and they killed several of them.
      돌   (몇)몇의, 여럿의
At last one of the Frogs put his head out of
마침내, 드디어   머리를 내밀다
the water and said, "Oh, stop! stop! I beg of you:
                              멈추다, 그만하다, 중단하다
what is sport to you is death to us."
          스포츠[운동/경기]   죽는 것, 죽음, 사망

31

MERCURY AND THE WOODMAN

A Woodman was felling a tree on the bank
나무꾼, 벌목꾼; 산지기 fall의 과거 둑, 제방
of a river, when his axe, glancing off the
강 도끼 …을 스치다, 빗나가다
trunk, flew out of his hands and fell into the wa-
나무의 몸통 날다(fly) 손 물 속으로
ter. As he stood by the water's edge lamenting
stand의 과거, 과거분사 물가 애통[한탄/통탄]하다
his loss, Mercury appeared and asked him the
분실, 상실 메르쿠리우스(상업의 신)의 영어 이름; 그리스 신화의 헤르메스에 해당
reason for his grief; and on learning what had
이유, 까닭 깊은 슬픔
happened, out of pity for his distress he dived
~이 일어나다 연민, 동정(심) (정신적) 고통, 괴로움
into the river and, bringing up a golden axe,
가져오다 황금의
asked him if that was the one he had lost. The
묻다 잃어버린
Woodman replied that it was not, and Mercury
대답하다
then dived a second time, and, bringing up a
다이빙하다 두 번째로 가져오다
silver axe, asked if that was his.
은도끼

"No, that is not mine either," said the Wood-
(부정문에서) …도
man.

Once more Mercury dived into the river,
다시 한 번 (물 속으로 거꾸로) 뛰어들다
and brought up the missing axe. The Woodman
잃어버린
was overjoyed at recovering his property, and
매우 기뻐하다, 기쁨에 넘치다 재산, 소유물
thanked his benefactor warmly; and the latter
감사하다 후원자, 은인 따뜻하게; 열렬히 후자
was so pleased with his honesty that he made
…을 기뻐하는, …이 마음에 드는 정직(성), 솔직함

him a present of the other two axes.

When the Woodman told the story to his companions, one of these was filled with envy of his good fortune and determined to try his luck for himself. So he went and began to fell a tree at the edge of the river, and presently contrived to let his axe drop into the water.

Mercury appeared as before, and, on learning that his axe had fallen in, he dived and brought up a golden axe, as he had done on the previous occasion. Without waiting to be asked whether it was his or not the fellow cried, "That's mine, that's mine," and stretched out his hand eagerly for the prize: but Mercury was so disgusted at his dishonesty that he not only declined to give him the golden axe, but also refused to recover for him the one he had let fall into the stream.

Honesty is the best policy.

THE CROW AND THE PITCHER

A thirsty Crow found a Pitcher with some
water in it, but so little was there that, try
as she might, she could not reach it with her
beak, and it seemed as though she would die of
thirst within sight of the remedy. At last she hit
upon a clever plan. She began dropping pebbles
into the Pitcher, and with each pebble the water rose a little higher until at last it reached
the brim, and the knowing bird was enabled to
quench her thirst.

Necessity is the mother of invention.

THE NORTH WIND AND THE SUN

A dispute arose between the North Wind
분쟁, 분규; 논란, 논쟁 ~사이에서 북풍

and the Sun, each claiming that he was
태양 (…이 사실이라고) 주장하다

stronger than the other. At last they agreed to
더 강한, 더 힘센 …에 대해 합의하다

try their powers upon a traveller, to see which
힘 여행자

could soonest strip him of his cloak.
가장 빨리 옷을 벗다[벗기다] 망토

The North Wind had the first try; and, gat
시도하다 모으다

hering up all his force for the attack, he came
(물리적으로 나타나는) 힘 공격

whirling furiously down upon the man, and
소용돌이 치는 미친 듯이 노하여[날뛰어], 광란하여; 맹렬히

caught up his cloak as though he would wrest
마치 …인 것처럼 비틀어 떼다

it from him by one single effort: but the harder
수고, 노력 더 심한

he blew, the more closely the man wrapped it
꽉, 단단히, 빽빽이 싸다, 둘러싸다

round himself. Then came the turn of the Sun.
차례, 순서

At first he beamed gently upon the traveller,
처음에, 맨 먼저 빛줄기를 비추다 다정하게, 부드럽게

who soon unclasped his cloak and walked on
곧, 이내 (쥐었던 양손 등을) 펴다 걸어가다

with it hanging loosely about his shoulders:
느슨하게, 헐겁게 어깨

then he shone forth in his full strength, and the
빛나다(shine) …쪽으로, 앞으로 힘, 기운

man, before he had gone many steps, was glad
기꺼이 ~하다

to throw his cloak right off and complete his
내던지다 즉각, 곧

journey more lightly clad.
여행, 여정 차려입은

Persuasion is better than force.
설득   ~보다 낫다   물리력, 폭력

THE MISTRESS AND HER SERVANTS

A Widow, thrifty and industrious, had two
미망인, 과부   절약하는   근면한, 부지런한
servants, whom she kept pretty hard at
하인, 종   아주, 매우 열심히, 힘껏
work. They were not allowed to lie long abed
              허락하다, 용납하다   잠자리에 누워 있는
in the mornings, but the old lady had them up
and doing as soon as the cock crew. They dis-
          ···하자마자, ···하자 곧   수탉   꼬끼오 하고 울다(crow)
liked intensely having to get up at such an hour,
      몹시, 극심하게   (잠자리에서) 일어나다[~를 깨우다]
especially in winter-time: and they thought
특히, 특별하게   겨울철에
that if it were not for the cock waking up their
                              수탉   잠을 깨우다
Mistress so horribly early, they could sleep lon-
여주인   지독하게, 끔찍하게   (잠을) 자다
ger. So they caught it and wrung its neck. But
                          목을 비틀다(wring)
they weren't prepared for the consequences.
          ···에 준비[각오]가 된   (발생한 일의) 결과
For what happened was that their Mistress, not
hearing the cock crow as usual, waked them up
                        늘 그렇듯이[평상시처럼]
earlier than ever, and set them to work in the
전보다 더 일찍
middle of the night.
한밤중, 심야

THE WOLF IN SHEEP'S CLOTHING

A Wolf resolved to disguise himself in order
늑대, 이리 (문제 등을) 해결하다 변장하다, 가장하다, 위장하다
that he might prey upon a flock of sheep
먹이, 사냥감; 희생자   무리, 떼   양
without fear of detection. So he clothed himself
공포, 두려움 발견, 간파, 탐지   옷을 입히다
in a sheepskin, and slipped among the sheep
(양털이 그대로 있는) 양가죽 ~사이로 미끄러져 들어가다
when they were out at pasture. He completely
초원, 목초지   완전히, 전적으로
deceived the shepherd, and when the flock was
속이다, 기만하다   양치기
penned for the night he was shut in with the
우리[축사] 안에 넣다   밤   갇히다
rest. But that very night as it happened, the
바로 그 밤에   (계획하지 않은 일이) 일어나다
shepherd, requiring a supply of mutton for the
필요로 하다   공급[비축](량)   양고기   식탁에 내놓을
table, laid hands on the Wolf in mistake for a
손을 대다   ~으로 잘못 생각하고
Sheep, and killed him with his knife on the spot.
죽이다   칼   즉석에서, 그 자리에서

THE GOODS AND THE ILLS

There was a time in the youth of the world
시간[때]; 시대[시기]   어린 시절; 젊음, 청춘
when Goods and Ills entered equally into
들어가다[오다]   똑같이, 동일[동등]하게
the concerns of men, so that the Goods did not
걱정, 염려, 관심사
prevail to make them altogether blessed, nor the
만연[팽배]하다; 승리하다[이기다]   완전히; 모두 합쳐   축성하다, 신성하게 하다
Ills to make them wholly miserable.
전적으로   비참한, 우울한
But owing to the foolishness of mankind the
갚아야 할[빚이 있는]   어리석음   인류; (모든) 인간, 사람들
Ills multiplied greatly in number and increased
다양한, 복합적인   대단히, 크게   증가하다, 인상되다
in strength, until it seemed as though they
힘, 기운   마치 ~인 것처럼
would deprive the Goods of all share in human
~에게서 (중요한) ~을 박탈하다[빼앗다]   나눔, 나눠 가지는 것
affairs, and banish them from the earth.
사건, 일   추방하다, 제거하다   지구
The latter, therefore, betook themselves
후자   그래서, 그러므로   가다(betake)
to heaven and complained to Jupiter of the
천국, 천당, 하늘나라   불평하다, 항의하다
treatment they had received, at the same time
(~에 대한) 대우[처우/처리]   받다, 받아들이다   같은 시간에, 동시에
praying him to grant them protection from the
기도하다[빌다], 기원하다   승인[허락]하다   보호(책), 보장
Ills, and to advise them concerning the manner
조언하다, 충고하다   …에 관한[관련된]   방식; 태도; 예의
of their intercourse with men.
교류, 교제, 소통
Jupiter granted their request for protection,
요청, 신청
and decreed that for the future they should not
명하다, 결정하다   미래, 장래
go among men openly in a body, and so be liable
터놓고, 드러내 놓고, 솔직하게

to attack from the hostile Ills, but singly and
공격하다 　　　　　 적대적인; (~을) 강력히 반대[거부]하는

unobserved, and at infrequent and unexpected
(남의) 눈에 띄지 않는 　　　 잦지 않은, 드문 　　 예상 밖의, 뜻밖의

intervals.
간격; 사이

　　Hence it is that the earth is full of Ills, for
　　이런 이유로 　　　　　　　　 ~으로 가득차다

they come and go as they please and are never
　　　　　　　　　　 (남을) 기쁘게 하다, 기분[비위]을 맞추다

far away; while Goods, alas! come one by one
멀리 떨어져 　　　　　 아아(슬픔·유감을 나타내는 소리)

only, and have to travel all the way from heaven,
　　　　　　　　 (장거리를) 여행하다

so that they are very seldom seen.
　　　　　　　　　 좀처럼[거의] …않는(=rarely)

THE FOX AND THE STORK

A Fox invited a Stork to dinner, at which the
초대[초청]하다   황새   (가장 주된) 식사[밥], 정식
only fare provided was a large flat dish
식사, 음식   제공[공급]하다, 주다   큰, 커다란 납작한 접시
of soup. The Fox lapped it up with great relish,
핥아 먹다, 게걸스럽게 먹다   즐거움[기쁨]
but the Stork with her long bill tried in vain to
길쭉하고 납작한 부리   헛되이
partake of the savoury broth. Her evident dis-
(제공된 것을) 먹다[마시다] 맛있는, 냄새 좋은 (걸쭉한) 수프, 죽 분명한, 눈에 띄는
tress caused the sly Fox much amusement.
교활한, 음흉한   재미, 우스움; 오락, 놀이

42

B
ut not long after the Stork invited him in
오래지 않아   초대하다, 초청하다
turn, and set before him a pitcher with a
차례, 순서   (목이 긴) 항아리[단지]
long and narrow neck, into which she could get
긴   좁은   목
her bill with ease. Thus, while she enjoyed her
쉽게, 손쉽게   이렇게 하여, 이와 같이   즐기다, 누리다
dinner, the Fox sat by hungry and helpless, for
배고픈   무력한, 속수무책인
it was impossible for him to reach the tempting
불가능한   닿다, 도달하다   맛있어 보이는
contents of the vessel.
내용물, ~속에 든 것   (액체를 담는) 그릇[용기/통]

THE MILKMAID AND HER PAIL

A farmer's daughter had been out to milk the cows, and was returning to the dairy carrying her pail of milk upon her head. As she walked along, she fell a musing after this fashion:

"The milk in this pail will provide me with cream, which I will make into butter and take to market to sell. With the money I will buy a number of eggs, and these, when hatched, will produce chickens, and by and by I shall have quite a large poultry-yard. Then I shall sell some of my fowls, and with the money which they will bring in I will buy myself a new gown, which I shall wear when I go to the fair; and all the young fellows will admire it, and come and make love to me, but I shall toss my head and have nothing to say to them."

44

Forgetting all about the pail, and suiting the
잊다, 잊어버리다   어울리는, 적합한
action to the word, she tossed her head. Down
행동, 동작   이야기, 말   머리를 홱 젖히다
went the pail, all the milk was spilled, and all
흘리다, 쏟다
her fine castles in the air vanished in a moment!
허황된 꿈[계획]   사라지다   단숨에, 순식간에

Do not count your chickens before they
            세다, 헤아리다   ~전에
are hatched.
부화하다

THE DOLPHINS, THE WHALES, AND THE SPRAT

The Dolphins quarrelled with the Whales,
and before very long they began fighting
with one another. The battle was very fierce,
and had lasted some time without any sign of
coming to an end, when a Sprat thought that
perhaps he could stop it; so he stepped in and
tried to persuade them to give up fighting and
make friends. But one of the Dolphins said to
him contemptuously, "We would rather go on
fighting till we're all killed than be reconciled by
a Sprat like you!"

THE FROGS' COMPLAINT AGAINST THE SUN

Once upon a time the Sun was about to
옛날 옛적에   태양   막 …하려는 참이다
take to himself a wife. The Frogs in terror
아내   개구리   깜짝 놀라서
all raised their voices to the skies, and Jupiter,
올리다; (목청을) 돋우다   하늘
disturbed by the noise, asked them what they
방해하다, 성가시게 하다   (듣기 싫은·시끄러운) 소리, 소음
were croaking about.
개골개골 울다

They replied, "The Sun is bad enough even
대답하다   안 좋은, 불쾌한, 나쁜 ~조차
while he is single, drying up our marshes with
단 하나의   바싹 말리다   습지
his heat as he does. But what will become of us
열기, 열
if he marries and begets other Suns?"
결혼하다   자식을 보다, 아비가 되다

THE FIR-TREE AND THE BRAMBLE

A Fir-tree was boasting to a Bramble, and said, somewhat contemptuously, "You poor creature, you are of no use whatever. Now, look at me: I am useful for all sorts of things, particularly when men build houses; they can't do without me then."

But the Bramble replied, "Ah, that's all very well: but you wait till they come with axes and saws to cut you down, and then you'll wish you were a Bramble and not a Fir."

Better poverty without a care than wealth with its many obligations.

THE DOG, THE COCK, AND THE FOX

A Dog and a Cock became great friends, and agreed to travel together. At nightfall the Cock flew up into the branches of a tree to roost, while the Dog curled himself up inside the trunk, which was hollow. At break of day the Cock woke up and crew, as usual. A Fox heard, and, wishing to make a breakfast of him, came and stood under the tree and begged him to come down.

"I should so like," said he, "to make the acquaintance of one who has such a beautiful voice."

The Cock replied, "Would you just wake my porter who sleeps at the foot of the tree? He'll open the door and let you in."

The Fox accordingly rapped on the trunk, when out rushed the Dog and tore him in pieces.

THE BEE AND JUPITER

A Queen Bee from Hymettus flew up to Olympus with some fresh honey from the hive as a present to Jupiter, who was so pleased with the gift that he promised to give her anything she liked to ask for.

She said she would be very grateful if he would give stings to the bees, to kill people who robbed them of their honey.

Jupiter was greatly displeased with this request, for he loved mankind: but he had given his word, so he said that stings they should have. The stings he gave them, however, were of such a kind that whenever a bee stings a man the sting is left in the wound and the bee dies.

Evil wishes, like fowls, come home to roost.

THE GNAT AND THE BULL

A Gnat alighted on one of the horns of
각다귀, 모기   (~에) 내려앉다   (양, 소 등의) 뿔
a Bull, and remained sitting there for
황소   계속[여전히] …이다
a considerable time. When it had rested
상당한, 많은   쉬다, 휴식을 취하다
sufficiently and was about to fly away, it said to
충분히, ~에 충분할 만큼   멀리 날아가다
the Bull, "Do you mind if I go now?"
              ~해도 괜찮을까?
The Bull merely raised his eyes and
              한낱, 그저, 단지 눈을 치켜 뜨다
remarked, without interest, "It's all one to me; I
언급[말/논평/발언]하다 관심, 흥미, 호기심 나한테는 매한가지다
didn't notice when you came, and I shan't know
        …을 의식하다[(보거나 듣고) 알다]   알다
when you go away."

We may often be of more consequence
            자주, 흔히, 보통   중요함
in our own eyes than in the eyes of our
            …자신의, …의
neighbours.
이웃 (사람); 옆에 있는 사람[것]

THE BLIND MAN AND THE CUB

There was once a Blind Man who had so fine a sense of touch that, when any animal was put into his hands, he could tell what it was merely by the feel of it.

One day the Cub of a Wolf was put into his hands, and he was asked what it was. He felt it for some time, and then said, "Indeed, I am not sure whether it is a Wolf's Cub or a Fox's: but this I know--it would never do to trust it in a sheepfold."

Evil tendencies are early shown.

THE BOY AND THE SNAILS

A Farmer's Boy went looking for Snails, and, when he had picked up both his hands full, he set about making a fire at which to roast them; for he meant to eat them.

When it got well alight and the Snails began to feel the heat, they gradually withdrew more and more into their shells with the hissing noise they always make when they do so.

When the Boy heard it, he said, "You abandoned creatures, how can you find heart to whistle when your houses are burning?"

THE FLEA AND THE MAN

A Flea bit a Man, and bit him again, and again, till he could stand it no longer, but made a thorough search for it, and at last succeeded in catching it. Holding it between his finger and thumb, he said--or rather shouted, so angry was he--"Who are you, pray, you wretched little creature, that you make so free with my person?"

The Flea, terrified, whimpered in a weak little voice, "Oh, sir! pray let me go; don't kill me! I am such a little thing that I can't do you much harm."

But the Man laughed and said, "I am going to kill you now, at once: whatever is bad has got to be destroyed, no matter how slight the harm it does."

Do not waste your pity on a scamp.

THE APES AND THE TWO TRAVELLERS

Two men were travelling together, one of whom never spoke the truth, whereas the other never told a lie: and they came in the course of their travels to the land of Apes.

The King of the Apes, hearing of their arrival, ordered them to be brought before him; and by way of impressing them with his magnificence, he received them sitting on a throne, while the Apes, his subjects, were ranged in long rows on either side of him.

When the Travellers came into his presence he asked them what they thought of him as a King.

The lying Traveller said, "Sire, every one must see that you are a most noble and mighty monarch."

"And what do you think of my subjects?" continued the King.

"They," said the Traveller, "are in every way

worthy of their royal master."
~의 가치가 있다; ~에 어울리다   국왕, 임금

The Ape was so delighted with his answer
                 많은 기쁨을 주다, 아주 즐겁게 하다   대답

that he gave him a very handsome present.
                          매우 훌륭한 선물

The other Traveller thought that if his
                                        만약 ~라면

companion was rewarded so splendidly for
동행, 동료, 친구   보상[보답/사례]하다   호화롭게, 화려화게

telling a lie, he himself would certainly receive
                                       틀림없이, 분명히

a still greater reward for telling the truth; so,
   더 큰, 더 대단한   진실, 사실

when the Ape turned to him and said, "And
              돌아서다, 돌아보다

what, sir, is your opinion?" he replied, "I think
                          의견, 견해, 생각   대답하다

you are a very fine Ape, and all your subjects are
            매우 멋진[근사한, 건강한]

fine Apes too."
        ~도, 역시, 또한

The King of the Apes was so enraged at his
                                        격분하게 만들다(=infuriate)

reply that he ordered him to be taken away and
대답   명령하다, 지시하다   끌고 나가다

clawed to death.
(손톱, 발톱으로) 할퀴다

THE OAK AND THE REEDS

An Oak that grew on the bank of a
오크 나무, 떡갈나무   자라다   강둑, 제방; (언덕 등의) 비탈
river was uprooted by a severe gale
(나무·화초 등을) 뿌리째 뽑다   엄청난 강풍
of wind, and thrown across the stream. It fell
…너머로 내던져지다   개울, 시내
among some Reeds growing by the water, and
~사이로   갈대   ~가에서, ~옆에서
said to them, "How is it that you, who are so
frail and slender, have managed to weather the
(허)약한, 부서지기 쉬운   빈약한   용케 ~해내다[지내다]   날씨
storm, whereas I, with all my strength, have
폭풍, 폭풍우   반면, 한편   힘, 기운
been torn up by the roots and hurled into the
찢다, 뜯다(tear)   뿌리   (거칠게) 던지다
river?"

"You were stubborn," came the reply, "and
완고한, 고집스러운, 완강한   대답, 응답
fought against the storm, which proved stronger
~에 맞서서 싸우다   폭풍, 태풍   (…임이) 드러나다[판명되다]
than you: but we bow and yield to every breeze,
머리를 숙이다   양보하다   산들바람, 미풍
and thus the gale passed harmlessly over our
강풍, 돌풍   해치지 않고, 해를 입히지 않고
heads."

THE SHEPHERD'S BOY AND THE WOLF

A Shepherd's Boy was tending his flock near a village, and thought it would be great fun to hoax the villagers by pretending that a Wolf was attacking the sheep: so he shouted out, "Wolf! wolf!" and when the people came running up he laughed at them for their pains. He did this more than once, and every time the villagers found they had been hoaxed, for there was no Wolf at all.

At last a Wolf really did come, and the Boy cried, "Wolf! wolf!" as loud as he could: but the people were so used to hearing him call that they took no notice of his cries for help. And so the Wolf had it all his own way, and killed off sheep after sheep at his leisure.

You cannot believe a liar even when he tells the truth.

62

THE FISHERMAN AND THE SPRAT

A Fisherman cast his net into the sea, and
어부, 낚시꾼   던지다   그물   바다
when he drew it up again it contained
끌어올리다   다시   …이 들어 있다
nothing but a single Sprat that begged to be put
청어(과의 작은 유럽산 바닷고기)
back into the water.
~을 다시 제자리에 갖다 놓다

"I'm only a little fish now," it said, "but I
고작, 단지, 오직   물고기
shall grow big one day, and then if you come
자라다
and catch me again I shall be of some use to
잡다   소용이 되다
you."

But the Fisherman replied, "Oh, no, I shall
대답하다
keep you now I've got you: if I put you back,
유지하다, 지키다   ~을 다시 제자리에 갖다 놓다
should I ever see you again? Not likely!"
언제든[한번이라도](=at any time)   말도 안 돼! 어림 없는 소리!

THE FOX AND THE GOAT

A Fox fell into a well and was unable to get
~속으로 떨어지다   우물, 샘   …할 수 없는   빠져나가다
out again. By and by a thirsty Goat came
머지않아, 곧   목이 마른, 갈증이 나는   들르다
by, and seeing the Fox in the well asked him if
묻다   ~인지 아닌지
the water was good.
물   (질적으로) 좋은

"Good?" said the Fox, "it's the best water I
최고의, 최상의
ever tasted in all my life. Come down and try it
맛보다   평생, 일생   내려오다   먹어보다
yourself."

The Goat thought of nothing but the pros-
염소   (어떤 일이 있을) 가망
pect of quenching his thirst, and jumped in at
(갈증을) 풀기, 담금질   갈증, 목마름   뛰어들다   즉시, 당장
once. When he had had enough to drink, he
충분히   마시다
looked about, like the Fox, for some way of get-
(…의) 주변을 둘러보다   빠져나갈 방법
ting out, but could find none.
아무 것도 없는
Presently the Fox said, "I have an idea. You
곧, 이내   발상, 생각, 방안, 계획
stand on your hind legs, and plant your forelegs
서다   뒷다리   (단단히) 놓다[두다]   앞다리
firmly against the side of the well, and then I'll
단단히, 굳게 … 가까이, …에 붙여[맞아]
climb on to your back, and, from there, by step-
오르다, 올라가다   등
ping on your horns, I can get out. And when I'm
뿔   밖으로 빠져나가다
out, I'll help you out too."
도와주다   ~도, 역시

64

The Goat did as he was requested, and the
요청하다, 요구하다
Fox climbed on to his back and so out of the
올라가다, 등반하다
well; and then he coolly walked away.
쌀쌀맞게, 태연하게, 침착하게
The Goat called loudly after him and re-
부르다   큰소리로   상기시키다
minded him of his promise to help him out: but
약속   도와주다
the Fox merely turned and said, "If you had as
고작, 그저, 단지 돌아서다, 돌아보다
much sense in your head as you have hair in
~감, 분별력   머리(털), 털
your beard you wouldn't have got into the well
(턱)수염
without making certain that you could get out

again."

Look before your leap.
보다, 바라[쳐다]보다   높이[멀리]뛰기, 도약

THE CRAB AND HIS MOTHER

An Old Crab said to her son, "Why do
크랩, 게   아들   왜, 어째서
you walk sideways like that, my son?
걷다   옆으로, 모로
You ought to walk straight."
…해야 하다   똑바로, 곧게
The Young Crab replied, "Show me how,
어린, 젊은   대답하다   (…을 분명히) 보여 주다
dear mother, and I'll follow your example."
따라가다, 따르다   본보기, 모범, 본
The Old Crab tried, but tried in vain, and
시도하다   헛되이, 아무 소용 없이
then saw how foolish she had been to find fault
어리석은, 바보 같은 (기분이 들게 하는)   잘못, 흠
with her child.

Example is better than precept.
실행은 교훈보다 낫다   (행동) 수칙, 계율

THE DOG AND THE COOK

A rich man once invited a number of his friends and acquaintances to a banquet. His dog thought it would be a good opportunity to invite another Dog, a friend of his; so he went to him and said, "My master is giving a feast: there'll be a fine spread, so come and dine with me to-night."

The Dog thus invited came, and when he saw the preparations being made in the kitchen he said to himself, "My word, I'm in luck: I'll take care to eat enough to-night to last me two or three days."

At the same time he wagged his tail briskly, by way of showing his friend how delighted he was to have been asked.

But just then the Cook caught sight of him, and, in his annoyance at seeing a strange Dog in the kitchen, caught him up by the hind legs and threw him out of the window.

68

He had a nasty fall, and limped away as
끔찍한, 위험한, 험악한, 심각한   절름거리며 떠나가다
quickly as he could, howling dismally.
최대한 빨리   (길게) 울다[울부짖다]우울하게, 으쓱하게
Presently some other dogs met him, and
곧, 이내, 머지않아   만나다
said, "Well, what sort of a dinner did you get?"
                   종류, 부류, 유형   만찬, 식사
To which he replied, "I had a splendid time:
          대답하다   아주 인상적인, 화려한
the wine was so good, and I drank so much of it,
와인, 포도주   마시다
that I really don't remember how I got out of the
         정말로, 실제로   기억하다   ~밖으로 나오다
house!"
집

Be shy of favours bestowed at the expense
부끄러운   호의, 친절   하사하다, 수여하다   돈, 비용
of others.

69

THE FARMER AND HIS SONS

A Farmer, being at death's door, and desiring to impart to his Sons a secret of much moment, called them round him and said, "My sons, I am shortly about to die; I would have you know, therefore, that in my vineyard there lies a hidden treasure. Dig, and you will find it."

As soon as their father was dead, the Sons took spade and fork and turned up the soil of the vineyard over and over again, in their search for the treasure which they supposed to lie buried there.

They found none, however: but the vines, after so thorough a digging, produced a crop such as had never before been seen.

THE MONKEY AS KING

At a gathering of all the animals the Monkey danced and delighted them so much that they made him their King. The Fox, however, was very much disgusted at the promotion of the Monkey: so having one day found a trap with a piece of meat in it, he took the Monkey there and said to him, "Here is a dainty morsel I have found, sire; I did not take it myself, because I thought it ought to be reserved for you, our King. Will you be pleased to accept it?"

The Monkey made at once for the meat and got caught in the trap. Then he bitterly reproached the Fox for leading him into danger; but the Fox only laughed and said, "O Monkey, you call yourself King of the Beasts and haven't more sense than to be taken in like that!"

THE THIEVES AND THE COCK

Some Thieves broke into a house, and found
도둑(thief의 복수)   몰래 잠입하다

nothing worth taking except a Cock, which
…의 가치가 있는   (무엇을) 제외하고는[외에는]

they seized and carried off with them.
와락[꽉] 붙잡다   들고 나가다

When they were preparing their supper, one
준비하다   저녁 (식사)

of them caught up the Cock, and was about to
잡아 올리다   수탉   막 …하려는 참이다

wring his neck, when he cried out for mercy and
목을 비틀다   비명을 지르다   자비

said, "Pray do not kill me: you will find me a
제발(=please)

most useful bird, for I rouse honest men to their
유용한, 쓸모 있는   정직한, 성실한

work in the morning by my crowing."
닭 울음소리

But the Thief replied with some heat, "Yes, I
도둑   열 받아서, 맹렬하게

know you do, making it still harder for us to get
더 열심히

a livelihood. Into the pot you go!"
생계수단, 밥벌이   (둥글고 속이 깊은) 냄비, 솥

THE FARMER AND FORTUNE

A Farmer was ploughing one day on his
farm when he turned up a pot of golden
coins with his plough. He was overjoyed at his
discovery, and from that time forth made an of-
fering daily at the shrine of the Goddess of the
Earth.

Fortune was displeased at this, and came to
him and said, "My man, why do you give Earth
the credit for the gift which I bestowed upon
you? You never thought of thanking me for your
good luck; but should you be unlucky enough
to lose what you have gained I know very well
that I, Fortune, should then come in for all the
blame."

Show gratitude where gratitude is due.

JUPITER AND THE MONKEY

Jupiter issued a proclamation to all the
발표[공표]하다　선언서, 성명서
beasts, and offered a prize to the one who,
짐승, 야수　주다, 제공하다　상
in his judgment, produced the most beautiful
판단, 심판, 심사, 감정, 평가; 추정　가장　아름다운
offspring.
(동식물의) 새끼

Among the rest came the Monkey, carrying a
…중에서　들고 있다, 나르다
baby monkey in her arms, a hairless, flat-nosed
팔　머리카락이 없는　납작코의
little fright.

When they saw it, the gods all burst into peal
보다　신　폭소를 터뜨리다
on peal of laughter; but the Monkey hugged her
껴안다, 포옹하다
little one to her, and said, "Jupiter may give the
prize to whomsoever he likes: but I shall always
누구든 …　늘, 언제나
think my baby the most beautiful of them all."

FATHER AND SONS

A certain man had several Sons who were
어느, 어떤   (몇)몇의, 여럿의
always quarrelling with one another,
        티격태격하다, 다투다
and, try as he might, he could not get them to
        아무리 애를 써도
live together in harmony. So he determined to
     함께   어우러지다, 조화를 이루다   결정하다
convince them of their folly by the following
납득시키다, 확신시키다   어리석음, 어리석은 행동
means.

Bidding them fetch a bundle of sticks, he
(…하라고) 말하다[명령하다]   가지고 오다   꾸러미, 묶음   막대기, 나뭇가지
invited each in turn to break it across his knee.
(정식으로) 요청하다   차례로   깨다, 부수다   무릎
All tried and all failed: and then he undid the
              실패하다   풀다: undo의 과거
bundle, and handed them the sticks one by one,
              건네주다   하나하나씩
when they had no difficulty at all in breaking
                      어려움, 곤란   부숨, 부러뜨림
them.

"There, my boys," said he, "united you will
                                연합하다, 결속하다
be more than a match for your enemies: but if
   ~보다 더   적
you quarrel and separate, your weakness will
   싸우다, 다투다   갈라지다, 헤어지다, (따로) 떨어지다   약점
put you at the mercy of those who attack you."
              고마운[다행스러운] 일   공격하다

Union is strength.
단결, 연합   힘, 강함

THE LAMP

A Lamp, well filled with oil, burned with a clear and steady light, and began to swell with pride and boast that it shone more brightly than the sun himself.

Just then a puff of wind came and blew it out. Some one struck a match and lit it again, and said, "You just keep alight, and never mind the sun. Why, even the stars never need to be relit as you had to be just now."

~으로 가득 차다　기름, 석유　불타다　선명한, 깨끗한　꾸준한, 한결같은　부풀다　자부심, 긍지　뽐냄, 자랑　빛나다(shine)　밝게, 눈부시게　바로 그때　한 줄기 바람　불어 끄다　치다(strike)　light의 과거　(~를) 유지하다　신경쓰지 마　심지어, ~조차　별　필요하다　…에 다시 점화하다　지금 당장은, 현재로서는

THE OWL AND THE BIRDS

The Owl is a very wise bird; and once, long ago, when the first oak sprouted in the forest, she called all the other Birds together and said to them, "You see this tiny tree? If you take my advice, you will destroy it now when it is small: for when it grows big, the mistletoe will appear upon it, from which birdlime will be prepared for your destruction."

Again, when the first flax was sown, she said to them, "Go and eat up that seed, for it is the seed of the flax, out of which men will one day make nets to catch you."

Once more, when she saw the first archer, she warned the Birds that he was their deadly enemy, who would wing his arrows with their own feathers and shoot them.

But they took no notice of what she said: in fact, they thought she was rather mad, and laughed at her.

When, however, everything turned out as
she had foretold, they changed their minds and
conceived a great respect for her wisdom.

Hence, whenever she appears, the Birds
attend upon her in the hope of hearing something that may be for their good. She, however,
gives them advice no longer, but sits moping
and pondering on the folly of her kind.

The Ass in the Lion's Skin

An Ass found a Lion's Skin, and dressed
당나귀 찾다[발견하다] 사자의 (동물의) 껍질 옷을 차려입다
himself up in it. Then he went about
쏘다니다, 누비다
frightening every one he met, for they all took
겁먹게[놀라게] 만들다 만나다(meet)
him to be a lion, men and beasts alike, and took
짐승, 야수 (아주) 비슷한
to their heels when they saw him coming. Elated
take to one's heels: 도망가다, 달아나다 마냥 신이 난
by the success of his trick, he loudly brayed in
성공 속임수, 장난 큰 소리로 (당나귀가) 울다
triumph. The Fox heard him, and recognised
대승을 거두어, 의기 양양하여 듣다(hear) 알아보다, 인식하다
him at once for the Ass he was, and said to him,
당장, 즉시
"Oho, my friend, it's you, is it? I, too, should
친구
have been afraid if I hadn't heard your voice."
무서워하다, 겁내다 ~라면 목소리

THE BOY BATHING

A Boy was bathing in a river and got out of
his depth, and was in great danger of being drowned.

A man who was passing along a road heard
his cries for help, and went to the riverside and
began to scold him for being so careless as to get
into deep water, but made no attempt to help
him.

"Oh, sir," cried the Boy, "please help me first
and scold me afterwards."

Give assistance, not advice, in a crisis.

THE QUACK FROG

Once upon a time a Frog came forth from
his home in the marshes and proclaimed
to all the world that he was a learned physician,
skilled in drugs and able to cure all diseases.
Among the crowd was a Fox, who called out,
"You a doctor! Why, how can you set up to heal
others when you cannot even cure your own
lame legs and blotched and wrinkled skin?"

Physician, heal thyself.

THE SHE-GOATS AND THEIR BEARDS

Jupiter granted beards to the She-Goats at
their own request, much to the disgust of
the he-Goats, who considered this to be an
unwarrantable invasion of their rights and
dignities.

So they sent a deputation to him to protest
against his action. He, however, advised them
not to raise any objections.

"What's in a tuft of hair?" said he. "Let them
have it if they want it. They can never be a
match for you in strength."

승인하다, 인정하다 (턱)수염 암염소 ··· 자신의 요청, 요구 혐오감, 역겨움, 넌더리 염소 사려하다, 고려하다, 숙고하다 부당한, 무법의 몰려듦, 쇄도, 침입 이권, 권리 위엄, 품위; 자존감 대표[사절]단 항의[반대]하다 ···에 반대하여[맞서] 충고하다, 조언하다 제기하다 어떤 이의, 반대 (이유) 머리 다발 ~하게 하다 원하다, 바라다 적수, 맞수 힘으로는, 힘에 있어서는

THE SWOLLEN FOX

A hungry Fox found in a hollow tree a
배고픈, 굶주린   (속이) 빈, 움푹 꺼진

quantity of bread and meat, which some
많은, 다량[다수]의   빵   고기

shepherds had placed there against their return.
양치기   놓다, 두다   …을 대비하여   돌아옴[감], 귀환

Delighted with his find he slipped in through the
아주 기뻐[즐거워]하는   미끄러지다, 미끄러져 내려[들어]가다

narrow aperture and greedily devoured it all.
좁은   (작은) 구멍   게걸스럽게   걸신 들린 듯 먹다

But when he tried to get out again he found
밖으로 (빠져)나오다

himself so swollen after his big meal that he
부어오른, 불어난   양이 많은[부담스러울 정도의] 식사

could not squeeze through the hole, and fell to
(좁은 곳에) 밀어[집어]넣다; (억지로) 비집고 들어가다

whining and groaning over his misfortune.
흐느껴 울다, 투덜대다   (고통·짜증으로) 신음[끙 하는] 소리를 내다   불운, 불행

Another Fox, happening to pass that way,
다른   지나가다, 통과하다

came and asked him what the matter was; and,
묻다   무슨 일인지

on learning the state of the case, said, "Well, my
상태   경우; 실정, 사실

friend, I see nothing for it but for you to stay
머물다

where you are till you shrink to your former
~까지   줄어들다   예전의, 옛날의

size; you'll get out then easily enough."
크기   쉽게

THE BOY AND THE NETTLES

A Boy was gathering berries from a hedge
모으다   산딸기류 열매   생울타리
when his hand was stung by a Nettle.
쏘다, 찌르다   쐐기풀
Smarting with the pain, he ran to tell his
욱신[따끔]거리다, 쓰리다   아픔, 통증, 고통   ~에게 달려가다
mother, and said to her between his sobs, "I
흐느껴 울다
only touched it ever so lightly, mother."
만지다, 건드리다   가볍게, 부드럽게
"That's just why you got stung, my son," she
said; "if you had grasped it firmly, it wouldn't
꽉 잡다, 움켜잡다   단호히, 막무가내로, 야무지게
have hurt you in the least."
다치게[아프게] 하다   조금도 …않다(not at all)

JUPITER AND THE TORTOISE

Jupiter was about to marry a wife, and deter-
막 ~하려는 참이다　(…와) 결혼하다　확정하다, 결정하다
mined to celebrate the event by inviting all
기념하다, 축하하다　행사　초대, 초청
the animals to a banquet.
(식물과 인간을 제외한) 동물　연회, 잔치

They all came except the Tortoise, who did
(~을) 제외하고는　거북
not put in an appearance, much to Jupiter's
~에 얼굴을 내밀다, ~에 나타나다
surprise. So when he next saw the Tortoise he
놀라움, 뜻밖의[놀라운] 일[소식]　그 다음[뒤]에
asked him why he had not been at the banquet.
묻다, 질문하다

"I don't care for going out," said the Tortoise;
…을 좋아하다　밖에 나가다, 외출하다
"there's no place like home."
곳, 장소　~처럼

Jupiter was so much annoyed by this reply
짜증나게[약 오르게] 하다　대답, 응답
that he decreed that from that time forth the
명하다, 결정하다
Tortoise should carry his house upon his back,
휴대하다, 가지고 다니다　등
and never be able to get away from home even if
~할 수 있다　…일지라도
he wished to.
바라다, 기원하다

THE DOG IN THE MANGER

A Dog was lying in a Manger on the hay
누워 있다, 눕다   (소·말의) 여물통[구유]   건초
which had been put there for the cattle,
놓다, 두다   소(집합적)
and when they came and tried to eat, he growled
시도하다   먹다   으르렁거리다
and snapped at them and wouldn't let them get
…을 덥석 물다, …에 달려들다
at their food.
식량, 음식, 식품; 먹이

"What a selfish beast," said one of them to
이기적인   짐승, 야수
his companions; "he can't eat himself and yet he
친구, 동료   그렇지만
won't let those eat who can."
(…하게) 놓아두다

THE OXEN AND THE AXLETREES

A pair of Oxen were drawing a heavily
짝, 한 쌍   황소(ox의 복수)   (마차·수레·자동차 등을) 끌다
loaded waggon along the highway, and, as
싣다, 태우다   짐마차   ~을 따라   고속도로, 공공 도로
they tugged and strained at the yoke, the Axle-
(세게) 끌어당기다 안간힘을 쓰다   멍에   굴대, 차축
trees creaked and groaned terribly.
삐걱거리다   신음 소리를 내다 끔찍하게
This was too much for the Oxen, who turned
(~에게) 너무 벅차다
round indignantly and said, "Hullo, you there!
분개하며, 분해서   여보세요(=hello)
Why do you make such a noise when we do all
소음, 시끄러운 소리
the work?"

They complain most who suffer least.
불평하다   시달리다; 고통받다

THE BOY AND THE FILBERTS

A Boy put his hand into a jar of Filberts, and
grasped as many as his fist could possibly
hold. But when he tried to pull it out again, he
found he couldn't do so, for the neck of the jar
was too small to allow of the passage of so large
a handful.

Unwilling to lose his nuts but unable to
withdraw his hand, he burst into tears.
A bystander, who saw where the trouble lay,
said to him, "Come, my boy, don't be so greedy:
be content with half the amount, and you'll be
able to get your hand out without difficulty."

Do not attempt too much at once.

THE OLIVE-TREE AND THE FIG-TREE

An Olive-tree taunted a Fig-tree with the
올리브 나무   놀리다, 비웃다, 조롱하다   무화과나무.
loss of her leaves at a certain season
분실, 상실   (나뭇)잎(leaf의 복수)   어느, 어떤 계절
of the year.

"You," she said, "lose your leaves every
모든, 매, 하나하나 다
autumn, and are bare till the spring: whereas I,
가을   벌거벗은, 헐벗은   봄   반면에, 한편
as you see, remain green and flourishing all the
계속[여전히] …이다   번창하다, 잘 자라다
year round."
일년 내내
Soon afterwards there came a heavy fall of
곧   나중에, 그 뒤에   폭설, 엄청나게 많이 내린 눈
snow, which settled on the leaves of the Olive
(떨어져내려) 앉다
so that she bent and broke under the weight;
구부러지다(bend)   무게, 체중
but the flakes fell harmlessly through the bare
눈송이   해롭지 않게, 피해가 없게
branches of the Fig, which survived to bear
나뭇가지   생존하다, 살아남다
many another crop.
작물, 수확물

THE FROGS ASKING FOR A KING

Time was when the Frogs were discontented
개구리 불만스러운, 불평하는
because they had no one to rule over them:
통치하다, 다스리다
so they sent a deputation to Jupiter to ask him
보내다 대표[사절]단 부탁하다
to give them a King.

Jupiter, despising the folly of their request,
경멸하다 판단력 부족, 어리석음 요청, 청원
cast a log into the pool where they lived, and
던지다 통나무 웅덩이, 연못 살다, 거주하다
said that that should be their King.

The Frogs were terrified at first by the splash,
(몹시) 무섭게[겁먹게] 하다 첨벙 소리
and scuttled away into the deepest parts of the
허둥지둥 달아나다 가장 깊은 부분
pool; but by and by, when they saw that the log
머지않아, 곧; 점점
remained motionless, one by one they ventured
계속[여전히] …이다 움직이지 않는, 가만히 있는 (위험을 무릅쓰고) 모험하다
to the surface again, and before long, growing
표면, 지면, 수면
bolder, they began to feel such contempt for it
대담하게 느끼다 경멸, 멸시
that they even took to sitting upon it.
심지어, ~조차

Thinking that a King of that sort was an
종류, 부류, 유형
insult to their dignity, they sent to Jupiter a
모욕   위엄, 품위; 자존감
second time, and begged him to take away the
두 번째   애원하다
sluggish King he had given them, and to give
느릿느릿 움직이는, 부진한; 둔한, 굼뜬
them another and a better one.
더 나은

    Jupiter, annoyed at being pestered in this
짜증이 난, 약이 오른   성가시게 하다[괴롭히다], 조르다
way, sent a Stork to rule over them, who no
황새   통치하다, 다스리다
sooner arrived among them than he began to
도착하다, 닿다
catch and eat the Frogs as fast as he could.
잡다   머다   빨리, 빠르게

THE LION AND THE BOAR

One hot and thirsty day in the height of
뜨거운, 무더운 목 마른, 갈증 나는 한여름에

summer a Lion and a Boar came down to
사자 야생돼지

a little spring at the same moment to drink.
샘, 옹달샘 같은 순간 마시다

In a trice they were quarrelling as to who
순식간에(=in an instant) 다투다, 언쟁을 벌이다, 싸우다

should drink first. The quarrel soon became a
싸움, 다툼

fight and they attacked one another with the ut-
(신체적인 힘을 이용한) 싸움 공격하다 최고의, 극도의

most fury.
분노, 격분

Presently, stopping for a moment to take
곧, 이내, 머지않아 잠시, 잠깐 한숨 돌리다, 잠깐 쉬다

breath, they saw some vultures seated on a rock
독수리, 콘도르 앉아 있다 바위

above evidently waiting for one of them to be
분명히, 명백하게 기다리다

killed, when they would fly down and feed upon
죽이다 내려앉다 ~을 먹다

the carcase.
(큰 동물의) 시체

The sight sobered them at once, and they
정신이 들게[냉정해지게] 만들다, 냉정[진지]해지다

made up their quarrel, saying, "We had much
(~와) 화해하다

better be friends than fight and be eaten by vul-
친구 싸우다 ~에게 먹히다

tures."

THE WALNUT-TREE

A Walnut-tree, which grew by the roadside,
가래나무, 호두나무   자라다   길가, 노변
bore every year a plentiful crop of nuts.
낳다, 생산하다(bear)   풍부한(=abundant)
Every one who passed by pelted its branches
                        지나가다, 통과하다   (돌 등을) 던지다   나뭇가지
with sticks and stones, in order to bring down
막대기   돌맹이   ~하기 위해서
the fruit, and the tree suffered severely.
열매, 과실   시달리다, 고통받다   극심하게, 심각하게
"It is hard," it cried, "that the very persons
                    외치다   (다름 아닌) 바로 그
who enjoy my fruit should thus reward me with
즐기다, 누리다, 향유하다   보상하다, 보답하다
insults and blows."
모욕(적인 말행동)   (손무기 등으로) 세게 때림, 강타

THE MAN AND THE LION

A Man and a Lion were companions on a
사자   동반자, 동행, 친구
journey, and in the course of conversa-
(장거리) 여행   …동안   대화; 회화
tion they began to boast about their prowess,
자랑하다, 뽐내다   (절묘한) 기량[솜씨]
and each claimed to be superior to the other in
(~이라고) 주장하다   (…보다 더) 우수한[우세한/우월한]
strength and courage. They were still arguing
힘   용기   논쟁하다
with some heat when they came to a cross-road
교차로
where there was a statue of a Man strangling a
조각상   교살하다, 목 졸라 죽이다
Lion.

"There!" said the Man triumphantly, "look
의기양양하여, 기세등등하게
at that! Doesn't that prove to you that we are
입증하다, 증명하다
stronger than you?"

"Not so fast, my friend," said the Lion: "that
너무   빠른; 빨리, 빠르게
is only your view of the case. If we Lions could
관점, 견해   (특정한 상황의) 경우
make statues, you may be sure that in most of
…의 대부분
them you would see the Man underneath."
…의 밑[아래/안]에

There are two sides to every question.
면   문제; 질문, 의문

98

THE TORTOISE AND THE EAGLE

A Tortoise, discontented with his lowly life,
거북   불만을 갖다, 불평하다   낮은, 하찮은
and envious of the birds he saw disporting
부러워하는, 선망하는   까불며 놀다
themselves in the air, begged an Eagle to teach
애원하다, 간청하다   독수리   가르치다
him to fly.
날다

The Eagle protested that it was idle for him
항의[반대]하다, 이의를 제기하다   쓸모 없는, 효과 없는
to try, as nature had not provided him with
자연; 천성, 본성   제공[공급]하다, 주다
wings; but the Tortoise pressed him with en-
날개   압박하다, 다그치다   간청, 애원
treaties and promises of treasure, insisting that
약속   보물   (…해야 한다고) 고집하다
it could only be a question of learning the craft
기술, 기교
of the air.

So at length the Eagle consented to do the
드디어, 마침내   동의하다, 허락하다
best he could for him, and picked him up in his
~을 집어 올리다
talons.
(맹금류의 갈고리 모양의) 발톱
Soaring with him to a great height in the sky
(하늘 높이) 날아오르다   아주 높은 곳
he then let him go, and the wretched Tortoise
놓아주다   가엾은, 불쌍한
fell headlong and was dashed to pieces on a rock.
거꾸로, 곤두박질쳐서   조각나다   바위

THE FOX WITHOUT A TAIL

A fox once fell into a trap, and after a strug-
떨어지다 함정, 덫 투쟁[고투]하다, 몸부림치다
gle managed to get free, but with the loss
용케 ~해내다 자유의 몸이 되다 상실, 분실
of his brush.
(여우의) 꼬리

He was then so much ashamed of his
(~여서[해서]) 부끄러운[수치스러운]
appearance that he thought life was not worth
(겉)모습, 외모 가치 있는
living unless he could persuade the other Foxes
…하지 않는 한, …이 아닌 한 설득하다
to part with their tails also, and thus divert
꼬리 (생각·관심을) 다른 데로 돌리다
attention from his own loss.
주의 (집중),주목; 관심, 흥미

So he called a meeting of all the Foxes, and
advised them to cut off their tails: "They're ugly
things anyhow," he said, "and besides they're
heavy, and it's tiresome to be always carrying
them about with you."

But one of the other Foxes said, "My friend,
if you hadn't lost your own tail, you wouldn't be
so keen on getting us to cut off ours."

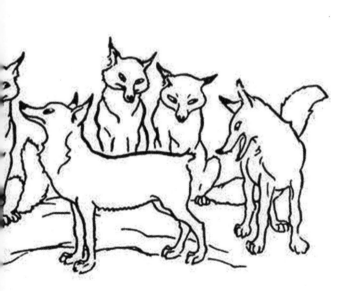

THE TRAVELLER AND HIS DOG

A Traveller was about to start on a journey, and said to his Dog, who was stretching himself by the door, "Come, what are you yawning for? Hurry up and get ready: I mean you to go with me."

But the Dog merely wagged his tail and said quietly, "I'm ready, master: it's you I'm waiting for."

THE WILD BOAR AND THE FOX

A Wild Boar was engaged in whetting his
tusks upon the trunk of a tree in the forest
when a Fox came by and, seeing what he was at,
said to him, "Why are you doing that, pray? The
huntsmen are not out to-day, and there are no
other dangers at hand that I can see."

"True, my friend," replied the Boar, "but the
instant my life is in danger I shall need to use
my tusks. There'll be no time to sharpen them
then."

THE SHIPWRECKED MAN AND THE SEA

A Shipwrecked Man cast up on the beach fell
난파한, 조난 당한   (해변으로) 떠밀어 올리다
asleep after his struggle with the waves.
잠들다   투쟁, 분투   파도
When he woke up, he bitterly reproached
잠에서 깨다, 정신 차리다 비통하게; 몹시 비난하다, 책망하다
the Sea for its treachery in enticing men with
배반, 배신   유도[유인]하다
its smooth and smiling surface, and then, when
매끄러운, 부드러운   표면, 지면, 수면
they were well embarked, turning in fury upon
(배에) 승선하다[승선시키다]   (격렬한) 분노, 격분
them and sending both ship and sailors to
둘 다(의)   배   선원, 뱃사람
destruction.
파괴, 파멸; 말살
The Sea arose in the form of a woman, and
일어나다(arise)
replied, "Lay not the blame on me, O sailor, but
책임, 탓
on the Winds. By nature I am as calm and safe
바람   선천[천성]적으로, 천성은; 본래   침착한, 차분한   안전한
as the land itself: but the Winds fall upon me
땅, 뭍, 육지   …에 닥쳐오다
with their gusts and gales, and lash me into a
세찬 바람, 돌풍   강풍, 돌풍   후려치다, 휘갈기다
fury that is not natural to me."
자연 발생적인, 정상적인, 당연한

MERCURY AND THE SCULPTOR

Mercury was very anxious to know in what estimation he was held by mankind; so he disguised himself as a man and walked into a Sculptor's studio, where there were a number of statues finished and ready for sale.

Seeing a statue of Jupiter among the rest, he inquired the price of it.

"A crown," said the Sculptor.

"Is that all?" said he, laughing; "and" (pointing to one of Juno) "how much is that one?"

"That," was the reply, "is half a crown."

"And how much might you be wanting for that one over there, now?" he continued, pointing to a statue of himself.

"That one?" said the Sculptor; "Oh, I'll throw him in for nothing if you'll buy the other two."

THE FAWN AND HIS MOTHER

A Hind said to her Fawn, who was now
암사슴   (생후 1년이 안 된) 새끼 사슴
well grown and strong, "My son, Nature
                                        자연
has given you a powerful body and a stout pair
                강한, 강력한, 힘센   튼튼한
of horns, and I can't think why you are such a
    뿔
coward as to run away from the hounds."
겁쟁이, 비겁자   도망치다, 달아나다   사냥개
Just then they both heard the sound of a
바로 그때   둘 다   듣다   소리
pack in full cry, but at a considerable distance.
    열렬히 울어대는, 한껏 울어대는   상당히 멀리에
"You stay where you are," said the Hind;
        머물다, 그대로 있다
"never mind me": and with that she ran off as
                                        달아나다
fast as her legs could carry her.
최대한 빨리

THE FOX AND THE LION

A Fox who had never seen a Lion one day
met one, and was so terrified at the sight
of him that he was ready to die with fear.
After a time he met him again, and was still
rather frightened, but not nearly so much as he
had been when he met him first.

But when he saw him for the third time he
세 번째로
was so far from being afraid that he went up to
…대신에, …라기보다는 반대로
him and began to talk to him as if he had known
시작하다   말하다, 이야기하다, 수다를 떨다
him all his life.
평생 동안

THE EAGLE AND HIS CAPTOR

A Man once caught an Eagle, and after
잡다: catch의 과거
clipping his wings turned him loose
깎아버리다   날개
among the fowls in his hen-house, where he
가금   닭장, 계사
moped in a corner, looking very dejected and
맥이 빠져 지내다   구석   실의에 빠진, 낙담한
forlorn.
쓸쓸해 보이는

After a while his Captor was glad enough
잠시 후   포획자, 억류자   기꺼이 ~하다
to sell him to a neighbour, who took him home
(돈을 받고) 팔다   이웃(사람)
and let his wings grow again.
날개   자라다

As soon as he had recovered the use of them,
~하자마자 곧   회복하다
the Eagle flew out and caught a hare, which he
밖으로 날아가다   토끼
brought home and presented to his benefactor.
가져오다   선물하다   후원자, 은인
A fox observed this, and said to the Eagle,
관찰하다
"Don't waste your gifts on him! Go and give
낭비하다   재능
them to the man who first caught you; make _
him_ your friend, and then perhaps he won't
아마, 어쩌면
catch you and clip your wings a second time."
잡다   자르다

110

THE BLACKSMITH AND HIS DOG

A Blacksmith had a little Dog, which used
대장장이 / 작은

to sleep when his master was at work, but
자다 / 일하고 있다, 근무 중이다

was very wide awake indeed when it was time
완전히 깨어 있는, 정신이 말똥말똥한 / 정말, 확실히

for meals.
식사, 끼니

One day his master pretended to be disgust-
어느 날 / 주인 / …인 척하다 / 혐오하다, 진저리나다

ed at this, and when he had thrown him a bone
던지다 / 뼈

as usual, he said, "What on earth is the good of a
평소처럼, 늘 그렇듯 / 도대체

lazy cur like you? When I am hammering away
게으른 / 똥개 / 망치질하다

at my anvil, you just curl up and go to sleep: but
모루 / 몸을 웅크리다[동그랗게 말다]

no sooner do I stop for a mouthful of food than
(음식) 한 입, 한 모금

you wake up and wag your tail to be fed."
꼬리를 흔들다 / 먹이를 먹다(feed)

Those who will not work deserve to starve.
일하다 / …을 (당)해야 마땅하다 / 굶어 죽다

THE DOG AND THE SHADOW

A Dog was crossing a plank bridge over a
(가로질러) 건너다 널빤지, (나무)판자 다리
stream with a piece of meat in his mouth,
개울, 시내 고기 한 덩어리 입
when he happened to see his own reflection in
우연히[마침] …하다[이다] (거울 등에 비친) 상[모습]
the water.
물

He thought it was another dog with a piece
또 다른
of meat twice as big; so he let go his own, and
고기 두 배[갑절]로 큰, 커다란 소유, 소유물
flew at the other dog to get the larger piece.
…에 덤벼들다(=attack) 더 큰, 더 커다란
But, of course, all that happened was that he
물론, 당연히
got neither; for one was only a shadow, and the
(둘 중) 어느 것도 …아니다 그림자
other was carried away by the current.
(나머지) 다른 사람[것] 조류에, 물살에

THE BEAR AND THE FOX

A Bear was once bragging about his gener-
ous feelings, and saying how refined he
was compared with other animals. (There is, in
fact, a tradition that a Bear will never touch a
dead body.)

A Fox, who heard him talking in this strain,
smiled and said, "My friend, when you are
hungry, I only wish you _would_ confine your
attention to the dead and leave the living alone."

A hypocrite deceives no one but himself.

THE ASS AND THE OLD PEASANT

An old Peasant was sitting in a meadow watching his Ass, which was grazing close by, when all of a sudden he caught sight of armed men stealthily approaching.

소작(농부), 소농(민) / 목초지 / 보다, 지켜보다, 주시하다 / 당나귀 / 풀을 뜯다 / 바로 옆에서, 근처에서 / 갑자기, 문득, 불현듯 / 무장한 / 몰래, 은밀히 / 다가오는, 가까이 접근하는

He jumped up in a moment, and begged the Ass to fly with him as fast as he could, "Or else," said he, "we shall both be captured by the enemy."

벌떡 일어나다 / 순식간에 / 애원하다, 간청하다 / 할 수 있는 한 빨리 / 둘 다 / 포로로 잡다, 억류하다; 포획하다

But the Ass just looked round lazily and said, "And if so, do you think they'll make me carry heavier loads than I have to now?"

주위를 돌아보다 / 느릿느릿하게 / 더 무거운 / 짐, 화물

"No," said his master.

주인

"Oh, well, then," said the Ass, "I don't mind if they do take me, for I shan't be any worse off."

상관없다, 괜찮다 / 데려가다 / 더 나쁜, 더 심한

THE MAN AND THE IMAGE

A poor Man had a wooden Image of a god, to which he used to pray daily for riches. He did this for a long time, but remained as poor as ever, till one day he caught up the Image in disgust and hurled it with all his strength against the wall.

The force of the blow split open the head and a quantity of gold coins fell out upon the floor. The Man gathered them up greedily, and said, "O you old fraud, you! When I honoured you, you did me no good whatever: but no sooner do I treat you to insults and violence than you make a rich man of me!"

THE OX AND THE FROG

Two little Frogs were playing about at the
개구리   놀다
edge of a pool when an Ox came down to
끝, 가장자리, 모서리   황소   내려오다
the water to drink, and by accident trod on one
물   마시다   우연히   디디다, 밟다(tread)
of them and crushed the life out of him.
으스러[쭈그러]뜨리다
When the old Frog missed him, she asked
놓치다, 잃어버리다   묻다
his brother where he was.
남자형제

"He is dead, mother," said the little Frog; "an
죽다　　　어머니　　　　　　　　작은, 어린
enormous big creature with four legs came to
막대한, 거대한　　　생명이 있는 존재, 생물　　　　다리
our pool this morning and trampled him down
　　　　　아침　　　　　　　　짓밟다, 밟아 뭉개다
in the mud."
　　　진흙, 진창

"Enormous, was he? Was he as big as this?"
　　　　　　　　　　　　　　　　　～만큼 큰
said the Frog, puffing herself out to look as big
　　　　　　　　　부풀리다　　　　　　　　　　　최대한 크게
as possible.

"Oh! yes, _much_ bigger," was the answer.
　　　　　　더 큰　　　　　　　대답, 회신, 대응
The Frog puffed herself out still more.
　　　　　　　　　　　　　　아직(도) (계속해서)
"Was he as big as this?" said she.

"Oh! yes, yes, mother, _MUCH_ bigger,"
　　　　　　　　　　　　　　　　big의 비교급
said the little Frog.

And yet again she puffed and puffed herself
　　　　　다시
out till she was almost as round as a ball.
　　　　　　　　　거의　　　　　둥근, 동그란, 원형의
"As big as...?"

she began-- but then she burst.
　　　　　　　　　　　　　터지다, 파열하다

119

HERCULES AND THE WAGGONER

A Waggoner was driving his team along a muddy lane with a full load behind them, when the wheels of his waggon sank so deep in the mire that no efforts of his horses could move them.

As he stood there, looking helplessly on, and calling loudly at intervals upon Hercules for assistance, the god himself appeared, and said to him, "Put your shoulder to the wheel, man, and goad on your horses, and then you may call on Hercules to assist you. If you won't lift a finger to help yourself, you can't expect Hercules or any one else to come to your aid."

Heaven helps those who help themselves.

120

THE POMEGRANATE, THE APPLE-TREE, AND THE BRAMBLE

A Pomegranate and an Apple-tree were
석류   사과나무
disputing about the quality of their fruits,
입씨름하다, 말다툼하다   질(質); 우수함, 고급   과일, 열매
and each claimed that its own was the better of
       (…이 사실이라고) 주장하다   더 좋은, 더 나은
the two.

High words passed between them, and a
격론, 언쟁; 극렬한 언사   ~사이에
violent quarrel was imminent, when a Bramble
폭력적인, 난폭한   (말)다툼, 언쟁 긴박한, 일촉즉발의, 목전의   검은딸기나무
impudently poked its head out of a neighbour-
건방지게(도), 경솔하게(도) 쿡 찌르다   이웃한, 인근의, 옆에 있는
ing hedge and said, "There, that's enough, my
생울타리, 산울타리   이제 됐다! 그쯤 해둬!
friends; don't let us quarrel."

THE BLACKAMOOR

A Man once bought an Ethiopian slave, who
had a black skin like all Ethiopians; but
his new master thought his colour was due to
his late owner's having neglected him, and that
all he wanted was a good scrubbing.
So he set to work with plenty of soap and hot
water, and rubbed away at him with a will, but
all to no purpose: his skin remained as black as
ever, while the poor wretch all but died from the
cold he caught.

THE LION AND THE WILD ASS

A Lion and a Wild Ass went out hunting together: the latter was to run down the prey
야생 당나귀 사냥하다
(둘 중에서) 후자
by his superior speed, and the former would
먹이, 사냥감
(…보다 더) 우수한[우세한/우월한] (둘 중에서) 전자
then come up and despatch it.
신속히 해치우다[처리하다]
They met with great success; and when it
성공, 성과
came to sharing the spoil the Lion divided it all
나누다, 나눠 갖다 약탈품, 전리품 (몫을) 나누다
into three equal portions.
부분, 일부; 1인분
"I will take the first," said he, "because I am
갖다, 가져가다 왜냐하면, ~때문에
King of the beasts; I will also take the second,
왕 짐승, 야수 또한, 역시
because, as your partner, I am entitled to half of
(사업) 파트너, 동업자 자격[권리]을 주다 ~의 반
what remains; and as for the third--well, unless
남다, 남아 있다 ~하지 않으면
you give it up to me and take yourself off pretty
~을 포기하다 아주, 매우
quick, the third, believe me, will make you feel
(재)빨리, 신속히 믿다
very sorry for yourself!"
유감스러운, 남부끄러운, 미안한

Might makes right.
힘, 세력, 권력, 실력 권리, 정의

THE EAGLE AND THE ARROW

An Eagle sat perched on a lofty rock,
독수리   앉아 있다[쉬다]   아주 높은, 우뚝한
keeping a sharp look-out for prey.
날카로운, 뾰족한, 예리한   먹이, 사냥감

A huntsman, concealed in a cleft of the
사냥꾼   감추다, 숨기다   (지면바위 등의) 갈라진 틈
mountain and on the watch for game, spied him
(아주 높은) 산   감시, 망 보기, 주시
there and shot an Arrow at him.
쏘다: shoot   화살

The shaft struck him full in the breast and
화살대   (세게) 치다, 부딪치다   가슴, 흉부
pierced him through and through.
꿰뚫다   완벽하게, 철저하게

As he lay in the agonies of death, he turned
극도의 (육체적·정신적) 고통[괴로움]
his eyes upon the Arrow.

"Ah! cruel fate!" he cried, "that I should
잔혹한, 잔인한 운명[숙명]
perish thus: but oh! fate more cruel still, that the
(끔찍하게) 죽다, 비명횡사하다   더, 더욱
Arrow which kills me should be winged with an
날아가다

Eagle's feathers!"
(새의) 털, 깃털

THE MAN AND THE SATYR

A Man and a Satyr became friends, and
사티로스(그리스 신화에서 숲의 신)
determined to live together. All went well
결정하다
for a while, until one day in winter-time the Sa-
잠깐은, 얼마 동안은   겨울철
tyr saw the Man blowing on his hands.
(입으로) 불다
  "Why do you do that?" he asked.
  ~하다   묻다, 질문하다
  "To warm my hands," said the Man.
  따뜻하게 하다, 데우다

That same day, when they sat down to
supper together, they each had a steaming hot
bowl of porridge, and the Man raised his bowl
to his mouth and blew on it.

"Why do you do that?" asked the Satyr.

"To cool my porridge," said the Man.

The Satyr got up from the table.

"Good-bye," said he, "I'm going: I can't be

friends with a man who blows hot and cold with

the same breath."

THE IMAGE-SELLER

A certain man made a wooden Image of
Mercury, and exposed it for sale in the
market. As no one offered to buy it, however, he
thought he would try to attract a purchaser by
proclaiming the virtues of the Image.
So he cried up and down the market, "A god
for sale! a god for sale! One who'll bring you
luck and keep you lucky!"
Presently one of the bystanders stopped him
and said, "If your god is all you make him out to
be, how is it you don't keep him and make the
most of him yourself?"

"I'll tell you why," replied he; "he brings gain,
it is true, but he takes his time about it; whereas
I want money at once."

THE WOLF, THE MOTHER, AND HER CHILD

A hungry Wolf was prowling about in search of food. By and by, attracted by the cries of a Child, he came to a cottage. As he crouched beneath the window, he heard the Mother say to the Child, "Stop crying, do! or I'll throw you to the Wolf."

Thinking she really meant what she said, he waited there a long time in the expectation of satisfying his hunger. In the evening he heard the Mother fondling her Child and saying, "If the naughty Wolf comes, he shan't get my little one: Daddy will kill him."

The Wolf got up in much disgust and walked away: "As for the people in that house," said he to himself, "you can't believe a word they say."

THE OLD WOMAN AND THE WINE-JAR

An old Woman picked up an empty Wine-jar which had once contained a rare and costly wine, and which still retained some traces of its exquisite bouquet. She raised it to her nose and sniffed at it again and again.

"Ah," she cried, "how delicious must have been the liquid which has left behind so ravishing a smell."

집어들다, 집어 올리다 · 비어 있는, 빈
와인병, 포도주병 · …이 들어 있다
진귀한, 희귀한 · 고가의, 값비싼 · (계속) 간직하다
자취, 흔적 · 매우 아름다운, 정교한 · (포도주의) 향미[향취]
들어올리다 · 코 · (킁킁거리며) 냄새를 맡다
몇 번이고, 되풀이해서
아주 맛있는, 냄새가 좋은, 풍미 있는
액체 · 뒤에
기가 막히게 아름다운(=gorgeous)

THE LIONESS AND THE VIXEN

A Lioness and a Vixen were talking together
about their young, as mothers will, and
saying how healthy and well-grown they were,
and what beautiful coats they had, and how they
were the image of their parents.

"My litter of cubs is a joy to see," said the
Fox; and then she added, rather maliciously,
"But I notice you never have more than one."

"No," said the Lioness grimly, "but that one's
a lion."

Quality, not quantity.
질(質); 우수함, 고급, 양질 (세거나 잴 수 있는) 양, 수량, 분량

THE VIPER AND THE FILE

A Viper entered a carpenter's shop, and went
from one to another of the tools, begging
for something to eat.

Among the rest, he addressed himself to the
File, and asked for the favour of a meal.

The File replied in a tone of pitying contempt, "What a simpleton you must be if you
imagine you will get anything from me, who
invariably take from every one and never give
anything in return."

The covetous are poor givers.

THE CAT AND THE COCK

A Cat pounced on a Cock, and cast about for some good excuse for making a meal off him, for Cats don't as a rule eat Cocks, and she knew she ought not to.

At last she said, "You make a great nuisance of yourself at night by crowing and keeping people awake: so I am going to make an end of you."

But the Cock defended himself by saying that he crowed in order that men might wake up and set about the day's work in good time, and that they really couldn't very well do without him.

"That may be," said the Cat, "but whether they can or not, I'm not going without my dinner"; and she killed and ate him.

The want of a good excuse never kept a villain from crime.

135

THE HARE AND THE TORTOISE

A Hare was one day making fun of a Tortoise for being so slow upon his feet.

"Wait a bit," said the Tortoise; "I'll run a race with you, and I'll wager that I win."

"Oh, well," replied the Hare, who was much amused at the idea, "let's try and see"; and it was soon agreed that the fox should set a course for them, and be the judge.

When the time came both started off together, but the Hare was soon so far ahead that he thought he might as well have a rest: so down he lay and fell fast asleep.

Meanwhile the Tortoise kept plodding on, and in time reached the goal. At last the Hare woke up with a start, and dashed on at his fastest, but only to find that the Tortoise had already won the race.

Slow and steady wins the race.

THE OXEN AND THE BUTCHERS

Once upon a time the Oxen determined to
옛날 예적에 　　황소(ox의 복수) 　결정하다
be revenged upon the Butchers for the
~에게 복수[보복]하다 　정육점 주인, 도살업자
havoc they wrought in their ranks, and plotted
대파괴, 큰 혼란[피해] 초래하다, 일으키다 　열, 줄, 정렬 　음모[모의]하다
to put them to death on a given day.
사형에 처하다 　　　정해진 날에, 날 잡아서
They were all gathered together discussing
모으다 　　　의논하다, 토론하다
how best to carry out the plan, and the more
수행하다 　　계획
violent of them were engaged in sharpening
폭력적인, 난폭한 　　…으로 바쁘다 　날카롭게[예리하게] 하다
their horns for the fray, when an old Ox got up
뿔 　　　싸움 　　일어서다
upon his feet and said, "My brothers, you have
남자 형제
good reason, I know, to hate these Butchers,
이유, 까닭, 근거 　몹시 싫어하다, 미워하다
but, at any rate, they understand their trade
어쨌든, 하여튼, 적어도 　이해하다, 알아듣다 　(특정한 유형의) 사업
and do what they have to do without causing
…을 야기하다
unnecessary pain. But if we kill them, others,
불필요한, 필요 이상의, 쓸데 없는 　　다른 사람들
who have no experience, will be set to slaughter
경험, 경력 　　(가축을) 도살하다
us, and will by their bungling inflict great suf-
서투른 　　(괴로움 등을) 가하다[안기다]
ferings upon us. For you may be sure that, even
though all the Butchers perish, mankind will
비록 …일지라도 　　　죽다, 소멸되다
never go without their beef."
소[쇠]고기

THE WOLF AND THE LION

A wolf stole a lamb from the flock, and was
늑대   훔치다, 도둑질하다(steal)   무리, 떼
carrying it off to devour it at his leisure
걸신 들린 듯 먹다
when he met a Lion, who took his prey away
만나다   먹이, 사냥감
from him and walked off with it.

He dared not resist, but when the Lion had
…할 용기가 있다, 감히 …하다
gone some distance he said, "It is most unjust
(공간상으로 떨어진) 거리   부당한, 불공평한
of you to take what's mine away from me like
빼앗아 가다
that."

The Lion laughed and called out in reply, "It
소리내어 웃다
was justly yours, no doubt! The gift of a friend,
틀림없이, 분명히   선물
perhaps, eh?"
아마, 어쩌면

THE SHEEP, THE WOLF, AND THE STAG

A Stag once asked a Sheep to lend him a
measure of wheat, saying that his friend
the Wolf would be his surety.

The Sheep, however, was afraid that they
meant to cheat her; so she excused herself, saying, "The Wolf is in the habit of seizing what he
wants and running off with it without paying,
and you, too, can run much faster than I. So
how shall I be able to come up with either of you
when the debt falls due?"

Two blacks do not make a white.

140

THE LION AND THE THREE BULLS

Three Bulls were grazing in a meadow, and were watched by a Lion, who longed to capture and devour them, but who felt that he was no match for the three so long as they kept together.

So he began by false whispers and malicious hints to foment jealousies and distrust among them.

This stratagem succeeded so well that ere long the Bulls grew cold and unfriendly, and finally avoided each other and fed each one by himself apart.

No sooner did the Lion see this than he fell upon them one by one and killed them in turn.

The quarrels of friends are the opportunities of foes.

THE HORSE AND HIS RIDER

A Young Man, who fancied himself something of a horseman, mounted a Horse which had not been properly broken in, and was exceedingly difficult to control. No sooner did the Horse feel his weight in the saddle than he bolted, and nothing would stop him.

A friend of the Rider's met him in the road in his headlong career, and called out, "Where are you off to in such a hurry?"

To which he, pointing to the Horse, replied, "I've no idea: ask him."

THE GOAT AND THE VINE

A Goat was straying in a vineyard, and began to browse on the tender shoots of a Vine which bore several fine bunches of grapes. "What have I done to you," said the Vine, "that you should harm me thus? Isn't there grass enough for you to feed on? All the same, even if you eat up every leaf I have, and leave me quite bare, I shall produce wine enough to pour over you when you are led to the altar to be sacrificed."

THE TWO POTS

Two Pots, one of earthenware and the other of brass, were carried away down a river in flood. The Brazen Pot urged his companion to keep close by his side, and he would protect him.

The other thanked him, but begged him not to come near him on any account: "For that," he said, "is just what I am most afraid of. One touch from you and I should be broken in pieces."

Equals make the best friends.

THE OLD HOUND

A Hound who had served his master well for years, and had run down many a quarry in his time, began to lose his strength and speed owing to age.

One day, when out hunting, his master started a powerful wild boar and set the Hound at him.

The latter seized the beast by the ear, but his teeth were gone and he could not retain his hold; so the boar escaped.

His master began to scold him severely, but the Hound interrupted him with these words: "My will is as strong as ever, master, but my body is old and feeble. You ought to honour me for what I have been instead of abusing me for what I am."

THE LARK AND THE FARMER

A Lark nested in a field of corn, and was rearing her brood under cover of the ripening grain.

One day, before the young were fully fledged, the Farmer came to look at the crop, and, finding it yellowing fast, he said, "I must send round word to my neighbours to come and help me reap this field."

One of the young Larks overheard him, and was very much frightened, and asked her mother whether they hadn't better move house at once.

"There's no hurry," replied she; "a man who looks to his friends for help will take his time about a thing."

In a few days the Farmer came by again, and saw that the grain was overripe and falling out of the ears upon the ground.

"I must put it off no longer," he said; "This
very day I'll hire the men and set them to work
at once."

The Lark heard him and said to her young,
"Come, my children, we must be off: he talks
no more of his friends now, but is going to take
things in hand himself."

Self-help is the best help.

THE HOUND AND THE HARE

A young Hound started a Hare, and, when he caught her up, would at one moment snap at her with his teeth as though he were about to kill her, while at another he would let

go his hold and frisk about her, as if he were playing with another dog.

At last the Hare said, "I wish you would show yourself in your true colours! If you are my friend, why do you bite me? If you are my enemy, why do you play with me?"

He is no friend who plays double.

148

THE LION, THE MOUSE, AND THE FOX

A Lion was lying asleep at the mouth of his
den when a Mouse ran over his back and
tickled him so that he woke up with a start and
began looking about everywhere to see what it
was that had disturbed him.

A Fox, who was looking on, thought he
would have a joke at the expense of the Lion; so
he said, "Well, this is the first time I've seen a
Lion afraid of a Mouse."

"Afraid of a Mouse?" said the Lion testily:
"not I! It's his bad manners I can't stand."

THE WOLF AND THE CRANE

A Wolf once got a bone stuck in his throat. So he went to a Crane and begged her to put her long bill down his throat and pull it out. "I'll make it worth your while," he added.

The Crane did as she was asked, and got the bone out quite easily.

The Wolf thanked her warmly, and was just turning away, when she cried, "What about that fee of mine?"

"Well, what about it?" snapped the Wolf, baring his teeth as he spoke; "you can go about boasting that you once put your head into a Wolf's mouth and didn't get it bitten off. What more do you want?"

THE WOLF AND THE SHEEP

A Wolf was worried and badly bitten by
걱정하다, 마음을 졸이다   심하게   물다: bite의 과거분사
dogs, and lay a long time for dead.
누워 있다; 눕다   죽은
By and by he began to revive, and, feeling
머지않아, 곧; 점차   활기를 되찾다, 회복하다
very hungry, called out to a passing Sheep and
배고픈, 굶주린 부르다   지나가는   양
said, "Would you kindly bring me some water
              친절하게   가져다[제공해] 주다
from the stream close by? I can manage about
        시내, 개울   바로 옆에, 근처에   (어떻게든) …하다
meat, if only I could get something to drink."
                    어떤 것, 무엇   마시다
But this Sheep was no fool.
                바보 같은, 어리석은
"I can quite understand", said he, "that if
꽤, 잘   알다, 이해하다
I brought you the water, you would have no
가져오다(bring)
difficulty about the meat. Good-morning."
어려움, 곤경, 장애

THE THREE TRADESMEN

The citizens of a certain city were debating
about the best material to use in the
fortifications which were about to be erected for
the greater security of the town.

A Carpenter got up and advised the use of
wood, which he said was readily procurable and
easily worked.

A Stone-mason objected to wood on the
ground that it was so inflammable, and recom-
mended stones instead.

Then a Tanner got on his legs and said, "In
my opinion there's nothing like leather."

Every man for himself.

THE TOWN MOUSE AND THE COUNTRY MOUSE

A Town Mouse and a Country Mouse were
acquaintances, and the Country Mouse
one day invited his friend to come and see him
at his home in the fields. The Town Mouse
came, and they sat down to a dinner of bar-
leycorns and roots, the latter of which had a
distinctly earthy flavour. The fare was not much
to the taste of the guest, and presently he broke
out with "My poor dear friend, you live here no
better than the ants. Now, you should just see
how I fare! My larder is a regular horn of plenty.
You must come and stay with me, and I promise
you you shall live on the fat of the land."

So when he returned to town he took the
Country Mouse with him, and showed him into
a larder containing flour and oatmeal and figs
and honey and dates. The Country Mouse had
never seen anything like it, and sat down to

도시 시골
아는 사람, 지인; 친분
초대하다
들판, 벌판
앉다 저녁 식사 보리옥수수
(식물의) 뿌리 (둘 중에서) 후자
뚜렷하게, 명백하게 흙의 풍미; 멋, 정취 식사, 음식
맛, 미각, 입맛 손님, 하객, 내빈 이내, 곧 달아나다
여기(에서)
~보다 낫다 개미
식품 저장실 지속적인; 완전한(강조) 풍요로움
머물다 약속하다
뚱뚱한, 살찐, 비만인
돌아가다 데려가다
보여주다
…이 들어 있다 밀가루 귀리 가루 무화과
꿀, 벌꿀 대추

154

enjoy the luxuries his friend provided: but be-
즐기다   호화로움, 사치   제공[공급]하다, 주다
fore they had well begun, the door of the larder

opened and some one came in. The two Mice
열다   안으로 들어오다
scampered off and hid themselves in a narrow
날쌔게 달아나다   감추다, 숨기다(hide)   좁은
and exceedingly uncomfortable hole. Presently,
    극도로, 대단히   불편한, 불쾌한   구멍   곧, 이내
when all was quiet, they ventured out again;
                조용한, 고요한   위험을 무릅쓰고 밖으로 나가다
but some one else came in, and off they scuttled
    어떤 다른 사람   허둥지둥 달아나다
again. This was too much for the visitor.
                              방문객, 손님
"Good-bye," said he, "I'm off. You live in the
                          be off 떠나다, 도망치다
lap of luxury, I can see, but you are surrounded
환경[장소], 안락한 장소   둘러싸다, 에워싸다
by dangers; whereas at home I can enjoy my
    위험
simple dinner of roots and corn in peace."
단순한, 소박한   평화

155

THE WOLF, THE FOX, AND THE APE

A Wolf charged a Fox with theft, which he
기소하다, 고소하다   절도, 도둑질
denied, and the case was brought before
인정하지[받아들이지] 않다, 부인하다
an Ape to be tried.
유인원
When he had heard the evidence on both
증거, 증언   양쪽, 둘 다
sides, the Ape gave judgment as follows: "I do
판단, 심판, 심사, 감정, 평가; 추정
not think," he said, "that you, O Wolf, ever lost
what you claim; but all the same I believe that
주장하다, 요구하다, 요청하다   믿다, ~라고 여기다
you, Fox, are guilty of the theft, in spite of all
유죄의, (잘못된 일에 대해) 책임이 있는   …에도 불구하고.
your denials."
부인, 부정, 거절, 거부

The dishonest get no credit, even if they
정직하지 못함   신용, 인정   …이라고 할지라도
act honestly.
정직하게, 성실하게, 충실하게

157

THE EAGLE AND THE COCKS

There were two Cocks in the same farmyard,
수탉(rooster)   농장 안 마당
and they fought to decide who should be
싸우다(fight)   결정하다, 결정짓다
master.
주인, 명인

When the fight was over, the beaten one
싸움, 투쟁   끝나다, 마치다   두들겨 맞은
went and hid himself in a dark corner; while the
숨다, 감추다   어두운, 컴컴한   구석
victor flew up on to the roof of the stables and
승리자   날아오르다   지붕   마구간, (때로) 외양간
crowed lustily.
크게, 활기차게

But an Eagle espied him from high up in the
(갑자기 …을) 보게 되다
sky, and swooped down and carried him off.
하늘   급강하하다, 위에서 덮치다

Forthwith the other Cock came out of his
곧, 당장, 대뜸
corner and ruled the roost without a rival.
지배하다, 통치하다   홰   경쟁자, 경쟁 상대

Pride comes before a fall.
자부심, 긍지   추락, 떨어짐

THE FARMER AND THE FOX

A Farmer was greatly annoyed by a Fox, which came prowling about his yard at night and carried off his fowls.

So he set a trap for him and caught him; and in order to be revenged upon him, he tied a bunch of tow to his tail and set fire to it and let him go.

As ill-luck would have it, however, the Fox made straight for the fields where the corn was standing ripe and ready for cutting. It quickly caught fire and was all burnt up, and the Farmer lost all his harvest.

Revenge is a two-edged sword.

THE CROW AND THE SWAN

A Crow was filled with envy on seeing the
까마귀　~으로 가득차다　　부러움, 선망
beautiful white plumage of a Swan, and
아름다운　하얀색　깃털　　백조
thought it was due to the water in which the
생각하다　　…때문이다　　물
Swan constantly bathed and swam.
끊임없이, 거듭　(몸을) 씻다　수영하다
So he left the neighbourhood of the altars,
leave의 과거　　이웃 사람들　　제단
where he got his living by picking up bits of the
줍기
meat offered in sacrifice, and went and lived
고기　주다, 제공하다　제물, 희생물
among the pools and streams.
~사이에　연못, 웅덩이　개울
But though he bathed and washed his feath-
…인데도　　씻다　　깃털
ers many times a day, he didn't make them any
여러 번, 자주
whiter, and at last died of hunger into the bar-
마침내, 결국　죽다　굶주림, 배고픔
gain.

You may change your habits, but not your
바꾸다, 변화하다　버릇, 습관
nature.
본성, 천성, 자연

THE STAG WITH ONE EYE

A Stag, blind of one eye, was grazing close
수사슴 눈이 먼, 맹인인 풀을 뜯다; 방목하다
to the sea-shore and kept his sound eye
해안, 해변 건강한, 정상적인
turned towards the land, so as to be able to
(어떤 방향) 쪽으로, (어떤 방향을) 향하여
perceive the approach of the hounds, while
감지[인지]하다 접근 사냥개
the blind eye he turned towards the sea, never
돌다; 돌리다
suspecting that any danger would threaten him
의심하다 위험 위태롭게 하다, 위협하다
from that quarter.
구역[지구]

As it fell out, however, some sailors, coasting
쓰러지다, 떨어지다 선원, 뱃사람 연안 항행의
along the shore, spied him and shot an arrow at
~을 따라 ~을 염탐하다 쏘다 화살
him, by which he was mortally wounded.
치명적으로, 죽을 정도로 상처[부상]를 입히다
As he lay dying, he said to himself, "Wretch
가엾은 사람
that I am! I bethought me of the dangers of the
잘 생각하다, 숙고하다
land, whence none assailed me: but I feared
(…한) 곳에서 공격을 가하다 두려워하다
no peril from the sea, yet thence has come my
위험성, 유해함 거기에서, 그 뒤에
ruin."
붕괴, 몰락, 파멸

Misfortune often assails us from an
불운, 불행 흔히, 종종
unexpected quarter.
예상 밖의, 뜻밖의

THE COCK AND THE JEWEL

A Cock, scratching the ground for something to eat, turned up a Jewel that had by
chance been dropped there.

"Ho!" said he, "a fine thing you are, no doubt,
and, had your owner found you, great would his
joy have been. But for me! give me a single grain
of corn before all the jewels in the world."

THE FARMER AND THE STORK

A Farmer set some traps in a field which he had lately sown with corn, in order to catch the cranes which came to pick up the seed. When he returned to look at his traps he found several cranes caught, and among them a Stork, which begged to be let go, and said, "You ought not to kill me: I am not a crane, but a Stork, as you can easily see by my feathers, and I am the most honest and harmless of birds." But the Farmer replied, "It's nothing to me what you are: I find you among these cranes, who ruin my crops, and, like them, you shall suffer."

If you choose bad companions no one will believe that you are anything but bad yourself.

163

THE GRASSHOPPER AND THE ANTS

One fine day in winter some Ants were busy
맑은, 화창한　겨울　개미　바쁘게
drying their store of corn, which had got
말리다, 건조하다　비축[저장]량
rather damp during a long spell of rain.
축축한, 눅눅한　…동안[내내]　(날씨 등이 계속되는) 기간

Presently up came a Grasshopper and
곧, 이내, 머지않아　베짱이
begged them to spare her a few grains, "For,"
간청하다　할애하다, 내어 주다　많지 않은, 적은
she said, "I'm simply starving."
굶주리다, 굶어 죽다

The Ants stopped work for a moment,
멈추다, 중단하다　잠시, 잠깐 동안
though this was against their principles.
~에 반하는, ~을 거슬러　(기본이 되는) 원칙

"May we ask," said they, "what you were doing with yourself all last summer? Why didn't
지난 여름
you collect a store of food for the winter?"
모으다, 수집하다(=gather)　음식, 양식

"The fact is," replied the Grasshopper, "I was
(…라는) 점, 사실
so busy singing that I hadn't the time."
(~하느라) 바쁜, (~에) 열심인

"If you spent the summer singing," replied
(시간을) 보내다[들이다]
the Ants, "you can't do better than spend the
~하는 게 더 낫다
winter dancing."
춤추다

And they chuckled and went on with their
낄낄거리다, 픽 웃다　계속하다
work.

164

THE FARMER AND THE VIPER

One winter a Farmer found a Viper frozen
겨울 농부 발견하다 독사 얼다
and numb with cold, and out of pity
추워서 감각이 없는 연민, 동정(심), 불쌍히 여김
picked it up and placed it in his bosom.
집어 들다 (조심스럽게) 놓다, 두다 가슴
The Viper was no sooner revived by the
되살아나다, 회생하다
warmth than it turned upon its benefactor and
따뜻함, 온기 은인, 후원자
inflicted a fatal bite upon him; and as the poor
상처를 입히다, 가해하다 치명적인, 돌이킬 수 없는 불쌍한, 가엾은
man lay dying, he cried, "I have only got what I
deserved, for taking compassion on so villainous
…을 받을 만하다[누릴 자격이 있다] 연민, 동정심 악랄한; 야비한
a creature."
생명체

Kindness is thrown away upon the evil.
친절, 호의 ~을 버리다; 허비하다 악, 악마

THE TWO FROGS

Two Frogs were neighbours. One lived in
개구리 이웃 (사람)
a marsh, where there was plenty of wa-
습지 ~가 많은[충분한]
ter, which frogs love: the other in a lane some
(나머지) 다른 하나 (시골에 있는 좁은) 길
distance away, where all the water to be had was
좀 떨어져서, 좀 멀리 떨어진 거리에
that which lay in the ruts after rain.
(부드러운 땅에 생긴) 바퀴 자국
The Marsh Frog warned his friend and
경고하다, 주의를 주다
pressed him to come and live with him in the
(~을 하도록) 압력[압박]을 가하다
marsh, for he would find his quarters there far
구역, 지구
more comfortable and--what was still more
편(안)한, 쾌적한 더 한층, 더욱 더
important--more safe.
중요한 안전한, 위험하지 않은
But the other refused, saying that he could
거절하다, 거부하다
not bring himself to move from a place to which
이사하다 곳, 장소
he had become accustomed.
~에 익숙해지다
A few days afterwards a heavy waggon came
나중에, 그 뒤에 짐마차
down the lane, and he was crushed to death un-
으스러[쭈그러]뜨리다
der the wheels.

THE BALD MAN AND THE FLY

A Fly settled on the head of a Bald Man and bit him. In his eagerness to kill it, he hit himself a smart slap. But the Fly escaped, and said to him in derision, "You tried to kill me for just one little bite; what will you do to yourself now, for the heavy smack you have just given yourself?"

"Oh, for that blow I bear no grudge," he replied, "for I never intended myself any harm; but as for you, you contemptible insect, who live by sucking human blood, I'd have borne a good deal more than that for the satisfaction of dash-ing the life out of you!"

THE MONKEY AND THE CAMEL

At a gathering of all the beasts the Monkey
모임, 회합   짐승, 야수   원숭이
gave an exhibition of dancing and
전시; (기교 등의) 발휘; (감정 등의) 표현[드러냄]
entertained the company vastly.
즐겁게 해 주다   손님, 함께 있는 사람들   대단히, 엄청나게

There was great applause at the finish, which
박수 (갈채)   마지막 부분, 끝
excited the envy of the Camel and made him
신이 난, 들뜬, 흥분한   부러움, 선망   낙타
desire to win the favour of the assembly by the
바라다, 원하다   집회, 모임
same means.

So he got up from his place and began danc-
일어나다   곳, 장소
ing, but he cut such a ridiculous figure as he
웃기는, 말도 안 되는, 터무니없는
plunged about, and made such a grotesque exhi-
(앞, 아래로 갑자기) 거꾸러지다   이상한, 기이한, 터무니없는
bition of his ungainly person, that the beasts all
(움직임이) 어색한[볼품없는]
fell upon him with ridicule and drove him away.
조롱, 조소

THE FLEA AND THE OX

A Flea once said to an Ox, "How comes it
벼룩   황소   왜? 어째서?
that a big strong fellow like you is content
큰   강한, 힘센 놈, 녀석   ~에 만족하다
to serve mankind, and do all their hard work for
섬기다   인류, 인간   힘든, 어려운
them, while I, who am no bigger than you see,
                              ~보다 더 큰
live on their bodies and drink my fill of their
~을 먹고 살다   몸, 육체   마시다
blood, and never do a stroke for it all?"
피   결코[절대/한 번도] … 않다

To which the Ox replied, "Men are very kind
대답하다   친절한
to me, and so I am grateful to them: they feed
고마워하는, 감사하는   먹이를 주다
and house me well, and every now and then
                              때때로, 가끔, 간간이
they show their fondness for me by patting me
도타운 사랑, 자애, 유난히 귀여워함 쓰다듬다, 토닥거리다
on the head and neck."

"They'd pat me, too," said the Flea, "if I let
쓰다듬다, 어루만지다
them: but I take good care they don't, or there
~을 잘 돌보다
would be nothing left of me."
아무것도[단 하나도] (…아니다·없다)

THE TRAVELLERS AND THE PLANE-TREE

Two Travellers were walking along a bare and dusty road in the heat of a summer's day. Coming presently to a Plane-tree, they joyfully turned aside to shelter from the burning rays of the sun in the deep shade of its spreading branches. As they rested, looking up into the tree, one of them remarked to his companion, "What a useless tree the Plane is! It bears no fruit and is of no service to man at all."

The Plane-tree interrupted him with indignation.

"You ungrateful creature!" it cried: "you come and take shelter under me from the scorching sun, and then, in the very act of enjoy-ing the cool shade of my foliage, you abuse me and call me good for nothing!"

Many a service is met with ingratitude.

THE BIRDS, THE BEASTS, AND THE BAT

The Birds were at war with the Beasts, and
새 / 전쟁, 전투 / 짐승, 야수
many battles were fought with varying
전투, 교전, 전쟁 / 가지각색의
success on either side.
성공; 성과 / 양쪽에서, 양면에
The Bat did not throw in his lot definitely
박쥐 / 확실히, 분명히
with either party, but when things went well
정당, 패, 무리
for the Birds he was found fighting in their
ranks; when, on the other hand, the Beasts got
열, 줄, 정렬 / 다른 한편으로는, 반면에
the upper hand, he was to be found among the
위쪽의, 상부의
Beasts.

No one paid any attention to him while the
주의 (집중),주목 / ~하는 동안
war lasted: but when it was over, and peace
지속되다 / 끝나다, 종결되다 / 평화
was restored, neither the Birds nor the Beasts
되찾게 하다; 회복시키다
would have anything to do with so double-faced
표리 있는, 위선적인, 이중적인
a traitor, and so he remains to this day a solitary
배반자, 반역자 / 남아 있다 / 외로운, 고립된
outcast from both.
따돌림[버림]받는 사람

THE MAN AND HIS TWO SWEETHEARTS

A Man of middle age, whose hair was turning grey, had two Sweethearts, an old woman and a young one.

The elder of the two didn't like having a lover who looked so much younger than herself; so, whenever he came to see her, she used to pull the dark hairs out of his head to make him look old.

The younger, on the other hand, didn't like him to look so much older than herself, and took every opportunity of pulling out the grey hairs, to make him look young.

Between them, they left not a hair in his head, and he became perfectly bald.

175

THE EAGLE, THE JACKDAW, AND THE SHEPHERD

One day a Jackdaw saw an Eagle swoop
갈까마귀 · 보다 · 독수리 · …을 내리덮치다
down on a lamb and carry it off in its
어린[새끼] 양
talons.
(갈고리 모양의) 발톱

"My word," said the Jackdaw, "I'll do that
아이고, 세상에, 저런
myself."

So it flew high up into the air, and then came
날아오르다 높이
shooting down with a great whirring of wings on
내려 꽂히다 · 씽 소리내며 날다[회전하다, 움직이다]
to the back of a big ram.
숫양

It had no sooner alighted than its claws got
(…에 날아가) 앉다 (=land) · 발톱
caught fast in the wool, and nothing it could do
단단히 고정된
was of any use: there it stuck, flapping away,
움직일 수 없는 · 날개를 퍼덕거리다
and only making things worse instead of better.
악화시키다 · ~대신에

By and by up came the Shepherd.
머지않아, 곧 · 다가오다 · 양치기

"Oho," he said, "so that's what you'd be doing, is it?"

And he took the Jackdaw, and clipped its
(꽉) 쥐다
wings and carried it home to his children.
나르다, 운반하다 · 아이들, 어린이들

It looked so odd that they didn't know what
이상한, 특이한

to make of it.

"What sort of bird is it, father?" they asked.
종류, 부류, 유형 (=kind)   묻다, 질문하다

"It's a Jackdaw," he replied, "and nothing
대답하다   오직, 그저[단지] …일 뿐인

but a Jackdaw: but it wants to be taken for an
원하다, 바라다

Eagle."

If you attempt what is beyond your power,
(힘든 일을) 시도하다, 애써 해보다 …저편에, ~너머

your trouble will be wasted and you court
버리다, 낭비하다

not only misfortune but ridicule.
불운, 불행   조롱, 조소

THE MILLER, HIS SON, AND THEIR ASS

A Miller, accompanied by his young Son,
방앗간 주인[일꾼]　동반하다, 동행하다
was driving his Ass to market in hopes of
몰다　당나귀　시장　희망, 소망
finding a purchaser for him.
구매자, 구입자
On the road they met a troop of girls, laugh-
(차가 다닐 수 있는) 도로[길]　무리, 떼　소녀, 아가씨
ing and talking, who exclaimed, "Did you ever
소리치다, 외치다
see such a pair of fools? To be trudging along
~한 쌍　바보　(지쳐서) 터덜터덜 걷다
the dusty road when they might be riding!"
먼지투성이인　(말을) 타다[몰다]

The Miller thought there was sense in what
생각하다(think)　일리가 있다
they said; so he made his Son mount the Ass,
아들　~에 오르다
and himself walked at the side.
걷다　옆에서

Presently they met some of his old cronies,
곧, 이내, 머지않아   (오랜) 친구
who greeted them and said, "You'll spoil that
맞다, 반기다, 환영하다   버릇없게 키우다
Son of yours, letting him ride while you toil
말에 타다   힘들게 ~하다
along on foot! Make him walk, young lazybones!
                                                                        게으름뱅이
It'll do him all the good in the world."

The Miller followed their advice, and took
~을 따르다   충고, 조언, 권고
his Son's place on the back of the Ass while the
                                                              등
boy trudged along behind.
(지쳐서) 터덜터덜 걷다

They had not gone far when they overtook
멀리 가다   추월하다, 앞지르다
a party of women and children, and the Miller
무리, 떼   여자, 부인   아이들
heard them say, "What a selfish old man! He
                                        이기적인
himself rides in comfort, but lets his poor little
              편안하게, 안락하게   가엾은, 불쌍한
boy follow as best he can on his own legs!"
뒤따라가다   다리

179

So he made his Son get up behind him. Further along the road they met some travellers, who asked the Miller whether the Ass he was riding was his own property, or a beast hired for the occasion.

He replied that it was his own, and that he was taking it to market to sell.

"Good heavens!" said they, "with a load like that the poor beast will be so exhausted by the time he gets there that no one will look at him. Why, you'd do better to carry him!"

"Anything to please you," said the old man, "we can but try."

So they got off, tied the Ass's legs together with a rope and slung him on a pole, and at last reached the town, carrying him between them.

This was so absurd a sight that the people
우스꽝스러운, 터무니없는
ran out in crowds to laugh at it, and chaffed the
사람들, 군중, 무리   놀리다, 농담하다
Father and Son unmercifully, some even calling
무자비하게, 매정하게; 엄청나게
them lunatics.
미치광이, 정신병자

They had then got to a bridge over the river,
다리, 교량   강
where the Ass, frightened by the noise and his
겁먹게[놀라게] 만들다   소음, 시끄러운 소리
unusual situation, kicked and struggled till he
특이한, 흔치 않은, 드문 상황   몸부림치다, 허우적[버둥]거리다
broke the ropes that bound him, and fell into
묶다(BIND의 과거·과거분사)
the water and was drowned.
물에 빠져 죽다, 익사하다

Whereupon the unfortunate Miller, vexed
그래서, 그 때문에, 그 결과   짜증난, 약오른
and ashamed, made the best of his way home
부끄러운, 창피한, 수치스러운
again, convinced that in trying to please all he
납득시키다, 확신시키다
had pleased none, and had lost his Ass into the
bargain.

THE STAG AND THE VINE

A Stag, pursued by the huntsmen, concealed himself under cover of a thick Vine. They lost track of him and passed by his hiding-place without being aware that he was anywhere near. Supposing all danger to be over, he presently began to browse on the leaves of the Vine. The movement drew the attention of the returning huntsmen, and one of them, supposing some animal to be hidden there, shot an arrow at a venture into the foliage. The unlucky Stag was pierced to the heart, and, as he expired, he said, "I deserve my fate for my treachery in feeding upon the leaves of my protector."

Ingratitude sometimes brings its own punishment.

THE SICK STAG

A Stag fell sick and lay in a clearing in the
수사슴 아픈, 병든 누워 있다(lie) (숲 속의) 빈터(=glade)
forest, too weak to move from the spot.
숲, 삼림 약한, 힘이 없는 움직이다, 이동하다 곳, 장소, 자리
When the news of his illness spread, a num-
소식 병, 아픔 퍼지다, 번지다
ber of the other beasts came to inquire after his
짐승, 야수 …의 안부를 묻다, 병문안을 하다
health, and they one and all nibbled a little of
(몸·마음의) 건강 조금씩[야금야금] 먹다
the grass that grew round the invalid till at last
풀, 잔디 자라다 ~주위에 (혼자 생활하기 어려운) 병약자
there was not a blade within his reach.
(한 가닥의) 풀잎 (팔을 뻗쳐 닿는) 거리[범위]
In a few days he began to mend, but was still
2, 3일 후에 회복되다, 낫다
too feeble to get up and go in search of fodder;
아주 약한, 쇠약한 찾아[살펴]보다 사료, 꼴, 먹이
and thus he perished miserably of hunger owing
죽다, 비명횡사하다 비참하게 굶주림 ~때문에
to the thoughtlessness of his friends.
생각이 모자람, 인정 없음

THE WOLF AND THE GOAT

A Wolf caught sight of a Goat browsing above
…을 찾아 내다, ~을 보다   염소   돌아다니다
him on the scanty herbage that grew on
빈약한, 보잘 것 없는 목초
the top of a steep rock; and being unable to get
가파른. 비탈진   ~할 수 없는, 불가능한
at her, tried to induce her to come lower down.
            설득하다, 유도하다   더 낮은
"You are risking your life up there, madam,
       (…을) 위태롭게 하다
indeed you are," he called out: "pray take my
정말, 참으로, 사실   소리쳐 부르다   제발
advice and come down here, where you will find
조언, 충고
plenty of better food."
많은 양의
The Goat turned a knowing eye upon him.
                      알고 있는   눈
"It's little you care whether I get good grass or
                    ~든 ~아니든   좋은, 훌륭한   풀, 잔디
bad," said she: "what you want is to eat me."
                              원하다, 바라다

184

THE HEIFER AND THE OX

A Heifer went up to an Ox, who was strain-
ing hard at the plough, and sympathised
with him in a rather patronising sort of way on
the necessity of his having to work so hard.
Not long afterwards there was a festival
in the village and every one kept holiday: but,
whereas the Ox was turned loose into the pasture, the Heifer was seized and led off to sacrifice.

"Ah," said the Ox, with a grim smile, "I see
now why you were allowed to have such an idle
time: it was because you were always intended
for the altar."

THE ASS AND HIS DRIVER

An Ass was being driven down a mountain road, and after jogging along for a while sensibly enough he suddenly quitted the track and rushed to the edge of a precipice. He was just about to leap over the edge when his Driver caught hold of his tail and did his best to pull him back: but pull as he might he couldn't get the Ass to budge from the brink. At last he gave up, crying, "All right, then, get to the bottom your own way; but it's the way to sudden death, as you'll find out quick enough."

당나귀 · 몰다 · 산길, 산간 도로 · 알맞은 속도로 천천히 달림 · 현명하게, 분별 있게 · 갑자기, 별안간 · 그만하다, 그만두다 · 돌진하다, 달려들다 · 끝, 가장자리, 모서리 · 벼랑 · 막 …하려는 참이다 · (높이길게) 뛰다, 뛰어오르다[넘다] · 운전자 · ~을 붙잡다 · 꼬리 · 잡아당기다 · 뒤로 · 약간 움직이다[움직이게 하다], 꼼짝하다 · 포기하다 · 맨 아래 (부분) · 갑작스러운 죽음; 돌연사 · …임을 알아내다, 발견하다

THE KINGDOM OF THE LION

When the Lion reigned over the beasts of the earth he was never cruel or tyrannical, but as gentle and just as a King ought to be.

During his reign he called a general assembly of the beasts, and drew up a code of laws under which all were to live in perfect equality and harmony: the wolf and the lamb, the tiger and the stag, the leopard and the kid, the dog and the hare, all should dwell side by side in unbroken peace and friendship.

The hare said, "Oh! how I have longed for this day when the weak take their place without fear by the side of the strong!"

THE LION AND THE HARE

A Lion found a Hare sleeping in her form, and was just going to devour her when he caught sight of a passing stag.
Dropping the Hare, he at once made for the bigger game; but finding, after a long chase, that he could not overtake the stag, he abandoned the attempt and came back for the Hare.
When he reached the spot, however, he found she was nowhere to be seen, and he had to go without his dinner.

"It serves me right," he said; "I should have been content with what I had got, instead of hankering after a better prize."

THE BULL AND THE CALF

A full-grown Bull was struggling to force his
huge bulk through the narrow entrance to
a cow-house where his stall was, when a young
Calf came up and said to him, "If you'll step
aside a moment, I'll show you the way to get
through."

The Bull turned upon him an amused look.
"I knew that way," said he, "before you were
born."

THE TREES AND THE AXE

A Woodman went into the forest and begged
나무꾼   숲, 삼림   간청하다
of the Trees the favour of a handle for his
              호의, 친절   손잡이
Axe.
도끼

The principal Trees at once agreed to so
        주요한, 주된   당장, 곧바로   동의하다
modest a request, and unhesitatingly gave him
겸손한, 보통의   서슴없이, 재빠르게, 확고하게
a young ash sapling, out of which he fashioned
어린 물푸레나무   묘목, 어린나무   (손으로) 만들다
the handle he desired.
                바랐던, 희망했던, 훌륭한

No sooner had he done so than he set to
                                                ~에 착수하다
work to fell the noblest Trees in the wood.
              가장 숭고한[고결한]
When they saw the use to which he was put-
                    사용, 이용
ting their gift, they cried, "Alas! alas! We are un-
        선물   외치다   세상에, 맙소사, 저런
done, but we are ourselves to blame. The little
                                …을 탓하다, … 때문으로 보다
we gave has cost us all: had we not sacrificed the
            (값·비용이) …이다   희생시키다
rights of the ash, we might ourselves have stood
for ages."

192

THE ASTRONOMER

There was once an Astronomer whose habit
천문학자 / 버릇, 습관
it was to go out at night and observe the
밤중에 / ~을 보다, 관찰하다
stars.
별

One night, as he was walking about outside
~를 돌아다니다 / 밖, 바깥
the town gates, gazing up absorbed into the sky
도시 / 문, 정문, 대문 / (관심을) 빼앗다, 빠지게 만들다
and not looking where he was going, he fell into
a dry well.
마른 / 우물

As he lay there groaning, some one passing
누워 있다 / 신음하면서 / 지나가다
by heard him, and, coming to the edge of the
우물가
well, looked down and, on learning what had
내려다보다 / ~를 듣다
happened, said, "If you really mean to say that
(무슨 일이) 일어나다 / 정말로, 실제로
you were looking so hard at the sky that you
열심히
didn't even see where your feet were carrying
~도, 조차 / 발(foot의 복수)
you along the ground, it appears to me that you
~을 따라 / 땅바닥, 지면 / ···인 것 같다(=seem)
deserve all you've got."
···을 받을 만하다

THE CAGE-BIRD AND THE BAT

A Singing-bird was confined in a cage which
노래하는 새   (~에) 넣다[가두다]   새장
hung outside a window, and had a way
매달다   ~의 바깥   창문
of singing at night when all other birds were
다른
asleep.
잠자다

One night a Bat came and clung to the bars
박쥐   꼭 붙잡다, 매달리다   창살
of the cage, and asked the Bird why she was
묻다
silent by day and sang only at night.
말을 안 하는, 침묵을 지키는, 조용한

"I have a very good reason for doing so," said
이유, 근거
the Bird: "it was once when I was singing in the

daytime that a fowler was attracted by my voice,
낮 (시간), 주간   들새를 잡는 사람, 새 사냥꾼
and set his nets for me and caught me. Since
그물   …한 이후로
then I have never sung except by night."
제외하고는

But the Bat replied, "It is no use your doing
~해도 소용없다
that now when you are a prisoner: if only you
재소자, 죄수; 포로
had done so before you were caught, you might

still have been free."
아직(도) (계속해서)

Precautions are useless after the event.
예방책, 예방 조치   소용없는, 쓸데없는   (중요한) 사건[일]

THE KID AND THE WOLF

A Kid strayed from the flock and was chased
길을 잃다[벗어나다]   무리, 떼   뒤쫓기다, 추적당하다
by a Wolf.

When he saw he must be caught he turned
round and said to the Wolf, "I know, sir,
that I can't escape being eaten by you: and so, as
my life is bound to be short, I pray you let it be
as merry as may be. Will you not play me a tune
to dance to before I die?"

The Wolf saw no objection to having some
music before his dinner: so he took out his pipe
and began to play, while the Kid danced before
him.

Before many minutes were passed the gods
who guarded the flock heard the sound and
came up to see what was going on.

They no sooner clapped eyes on the Wolf
than they gave chase and drove him away.

As he ran off, he turned and said to the Kid,
"It's what I thoroughly deserve: my trade is the
butcher's, and I had no business to turn piper to
please you."

THE BALD HUNTSMAN

A Man who had lost all his hair took to wearing a wig, and one day he went out hunting.

It was blowing rather hard at the time, and he hadn't gone far before a gust of wind caught his hat and carried it off, and his wig too, much to the amusement of the hunt.

But he quite entered into the joke, and said, "Ah, well! the hair that wig is made of didn't stick to the head on which it grew; so it's no wonder it won't stick to mine."

THE HERDSMAN AND THE LOST BULL

A Herdsman was tending his cattle when he missed a young Bull, one of the finest of the herd.

He went at once to look for him, but, meeting with no success in his search, he made a vow that, if he should discover the thief, he would sacrifice a calf to Jupiter.

Continuing his search, he entered a thicket, where he presently espied a lion devouring the lost Bull.

Terrified with fear, he raised his hands to heaven and cried, "Great Jupiter, I vowed I would sacrifice a calf to thee if I should discover the thief: but now a full-grown Bull I promise thee if only I myself escape unhurt from his clutches."

THE MULE

One morning a Mule, who had too much
아침   노새   너무 많은
to eat and too little to do, began to think
너무 적은   시작하다   생각하다
himself a very fine fellow indeed, and frisked
멋진, 근사한   정말로, 실제로   뛰놀다
about saying, "My father was undoubtedly
                          의심할 여지없이, 확실히
a high-spirited horse and I take after him
기개 있는, 활기찬   말   …을 닮다(=resemble)
entirely."
전적으로, 완전히, 전부
But very soon afterwards he was put into the
          나중에, 그 뒤에

harness and compelled to go
마구   강요하다, 강제하다
a very long way with a heavy
          먼 길   무거운 짐
load behind him.
          뒤에
At the end of the day,

exhausted by his unusual
기진맥진한, 진이 다 빠진, 탈진한
exertions, he said dejectedly to himself, "I must
노력, 분투   맥없이, 낙심하여
have been mistaken about my father; he can
          잘못 알고[판단하고] 있는
only have been an ass
                      당나귀
after all."

200

THE HOUND AND THE FOX

A Hound, roaming in the forest, spied a lion, and being well used to lesser game, gave chase, thinking he would make a fine quarry. Presently the lion perceived that he was being pursued; so, stopping short, he rounded on his pursuer and gave a loud roar. The Hound immediately turned tail and fled. A Fox, seeing him running away, jeered at him and said, "Ho! ho! There goes the coward who chased a lion and ran away the moment he roared!"

THE PACK-ASS AND THE WILD ASS

A Wild Ass, who was wandering idly about,
야생나귀 　　　　배회하다, 돌아다니다 한가하게, 게으르게
one day came upon a Pack-Ass lying at full
　　　만나다, 다가가다 집나귀 　 누워 있는
length in a sunny spot and thoroughly enjoying
길이 　　　화창한 곳, 장소 　　철저하게, 완벽하게 즐기는
himself.

Going up to him, he said, "What a lucky
가까이 가다 　　　　　　　　　　운 좋은, 행운의
beast you are! Your sleek coat shows how well
　　　　　　　　 (매끄럽고) 윤이 나는(=glossy)
you live: how I envy you!"
　　　　　부러워하다, 선망하다

Not long after the Wild Ass saw his acquain-
~뒤에 　　　　　　　　　　아는 사람, 지인
tance again, but this time he was carrying a
　　　 다시 　　　이번에는 　　나르다, 운반하다
heavy load, and his driver was following behind
무거운 짐, 화물 　　　　　　　~을 따라가다 ~뒤에서
and beating him with a thick stick.
때리다, 두드리다 　　　굵은, 두꺼운 막대기

"Ah, my friend," said the Wild Ass, "I don't

envy you any more: for I see you pay dear for
이제, 더 이상 　　　　　　　 납부하다, 지불하다
your comforts."
안락, 편안

Advantages that are dearly bought are
유리한 점, 이점, 장점 　　비싼 대가를 치르고
doubtful blessings.
의심스러운, …일 것 같지 않은 축복

THE ANT

Ants were once men and made their living
(과거) 언젠가[한때/한동안]
by tilling the soil. But, not content with
갈다, 경작하다(cultivate)   ~에 만족하다
the results of their own work, they were always
결과, 결과물   일, 작업   늘, 언제나
casting longing eyes upon the crops and fruits
(시선, 미소 등을) 던지다[보내다]   (농)작물   과일, 열매
of their neighbours, which they stole, whenever
이웃(사람)   훔치다(steal)
they got the chance, and added to their own
기회   더하다, 덧붙이다
store.
창고, 저장고, 보관소

At last their covetousness made Jupiter so
탐욕(스러움)
angry that he changed them into Ants. But,
화내다, 분노하다   바꾸다   개미
though their forms were changed, their nature
형태, 모습   본성, 천성
remained the same: and so, to this day, they go
남다, 남아 있다
about among the cornfields and gather the fruits
곡물을 재배하는 밭   모으다
of others' labour, and store them up for their
(육체적인) 노동[작업]   저장하다, 보관하다
own use.

You may punish a thief, but his bent
처벌하다, 벌주다   도둑   소질; 취향
remains.
(없어지지 않고) 남다

203

THE FROGS AND THE WELL

Two Frogs lived together in a marsh. But
one hot summer the marsh dried up, and
they left it to look for another place to live in: for
frogs like damp places if they can get them.

By and by they came to a deep well, and one
of them looked down into it, and said to the
other, "This looks a nice cool place: let us jump
in and settle here."

But the other, who had a wiser head on
his shoulders, replied, "Not so fast, my friend:
supposing this well dried up like the marsh, how
should we get out again?"

Think twice before you act.

THE CRAB AND THE FOX

A Crab once left the sea-shore and went and settled in a meadow some way inland, which looked very nice and green and seemed likely to be a good place to feed in.

But a hungry Fox came along and spied the Crab and caught him. Just as he was going to be eaten up, the Crab said, "This is just what I deserve; for I had no business to leave my natural home by the sea and settle here as though I belonged to the land."

> Be content with your lot.

THE FOX AND THE GRASSHOPPER

A Grasshopper sat chirping in the branches
of a tree. A Fox heard her, and, thinking
what a dainty morsel she would make, he tried
to get her down by a trick.

Standing below in full view of her, he praised
her song in the most flattering terms, and
begged her to descend, saying he would like to
make the acquaintance of the owner of so beautiful a voice.

But she was not to be taken in, and replied,
"You are very much mistaken, my dear sir, if
you imagine I am going to come down: I keep
well out of the way of you and your kind ever
since the day when I saw numbers of grasshop-
pers' wings strewn about the entrance to a fox's
earth."

THE ASS AND THE DOG

An Ass and a Dog were on their travels together, and, as they went along, they found a sealed packet lying on the ground. The Ass picked it up, broke the seal, and found it contained some writing, which he proceeded to read out aloud to the Dog. As he read on it turned out to be all about grass and barley and hay--in short, all the kinds of fodder that Asses are fond of.

The Dog was a good deal bored with listening to all this, till at last his impatience got the better of him, and he cried, "Just skip a few pages, friend, and see if there isn't something about meat and bones."

The Ass glanced all through the packet, but found nothing of the sort, and said so. Then the Dog said in disgust, "Oh, throw it away, do: what's the good of a thing like that?"

THE PIG AND THE SHEEP

A Pig found his way into a meadow where a
flock of Sheep were grazing.
The shepherd caught him, and was proceed-
ing to carry him off to the butcher's when he set
up a loud squealing and struggled to get free.
The Sheep rebuked him for making such a
to-do, and said to him, "The shepherd catches
us regularly and drags us off just like that, and
we don't make any fuss."
"No, I dare say not," replied the Pig, "but my
case and yours are altogether different: he only
wants you for wool, but he wants me for bacon."

THE GOATHERD AND THE GOAT

A Goatherd was one day gathering his flock
염소지기, 염소 돌보는 사람   모으다, 모이게 하다
to return to the fold, when one of his goats
돌아가다   (가축의) 우리(pen)   염소
strayed and refused to join the rest.
옆길로 새다   거절하다   합치다, 합류하다, ~에 끼다

He tried for a long time to get her to return

by calling and whistling to her, but the Goat
외침, 부르는 소리   호각[호루라기] 소리, 휘파람 소리
took no notice of him at all; so at last he threw a
주목, 관심, 집중   던지다
stone at her and broke one of her horns.
돌멩이   부러지다   뿔
In dismay, he begged her not to tell his mas-
실망, 경악   말하다 주인
ter: but she replied, "You silly fellow, my horn
어리석은, 바보같은
would cry aloud even if I held my tongue."
큰소리로, 크게   혀

It's no use trying to hide what can't be hid-
~해도 소용없다   숨기다, 감추다
den.

What's bred in the bone is sure to come

out in the flesh.

THE LION, JUPITER, AND THE ELEPHANT

The Lion, for all his size and strength, and
사자 크기 힘, 기운; 체력

his sharp teeth and claws, is a coward in
날카로운, 예리한 발톱 겁쟁이, 비겁자

one thing: he can't bear the sound of a cock
참다, 견디다 소리 수탉

crowing, and runs away whenever he hears it.
꼬끼오하고 우는 소리 도망가다, 달아나다 ~할 때마다

He complained bitterly to Jupiter for making
불평[항의]하다 격렬하게, 비통하게

him like that; but Jupiter said it wasn't his fault:
잘못, 실수

he had done the best he could for him, and,

considering this was his only failing, he ought to
(~을 ~로) 여기다; 고려하다; 참작하다 결점, 결함

be well content.
~에 만족하다

The Lion, however, wouldn't be comforted,
위로하다, 다독이다

and was so ashamed of his timidity that he
창피한, 부끄러운 겁 많음, 소심함

wished he might die.

In this state of mind, he met the Elephant
상태 마음 코끼리

and had a talk with him. He noticed that the
~와 이야기를 나누다 주목하다, 관심을 갖다

great beast cocked up his ears all the time,
짐승, 야수 위로 젖혀진, 위로 향하게 한 귀

as if he were listening for something, and he
경청하다, (귀 기울여) 듣다

asked him why he did so. Just then a gnat came
모기

humming by, and the Elephant said, "Do you see
윙윙거리는, 콧노래 부르는

that wretched little buzzing insect? I'm terribly
악마 같은, 비열한, 몹쓸 윙윙거리는 곤충 끔찍하게

afraid of its getting into my ear: if it once gets in,

~울 두려워하다   ~안으로 들어가다

I'm dead and done for."

죽다   끝장나다

    The Lion's spirits rose at once when he heard

정신, 영혼; 사기   당장, 즉시

this: "For," he said to himself, "if the Elephant,

huge as he is, is afraid of a gnat, I needn't be so

거대한, 어마어마하게 큰   ~할 필요가 없다

much ashamed of being afraid of a cock, who is

ten thousand times bigger than a gnat."

만 배   ~보다 더 큰

THE GARDENER AND HIS DOG

A Gardner's Dog fell into a deep well, from which his master used to draw water for the plants in his garden with a rope and a bucket.

Failing to get the Dog out by means of these, the Gardener went down into the well himself in order to fetch him up.

But the Dog thought he had come to make sure of drowning him; so he bit his master as soon as he came within reach, and hurt him a good deal, with the result that he left the Dog to his fate and climbed out of the well, remarking, "It serves me quite right for trying to save so determined a suicide."

THE RIVERS AND THE SEA

Once upon a time all the Rivers combined
옛날 옛적에　　　　　　　　　　　강　　　　결합하다
to protest against the action of the Sea in
항의[반대]하다, 이의를 제기하다　행동, 조치
making their waters salt.
짜게 만들다, 소금물로 만들다

"When we come to you," said they to the Sea,

"we are sweet and drinkable: but when once we
달콤한, 향기로운　　마실 수 있는
have mingled with you, our waters become as
섞이다, 어우러지다
briny and unpalatable as your own."
짠, 염분이 많은 (=salty)　입[구미]에 안 맞는
The Sea replied shortly, "Keep away from me
짧게　　　(~에[을]) 가까이 가지 않다[멀리 하다]
and you'll remain sweet."
(없어지지 않고) 남다; 계속[여전히] …이다

THE LION IN LOVE

A Lion fell deeply in love with the daughter
깊이, 대단히, 몹시   딸
of a cottager and wanted to marry her; but
(시골) 오두막에 사는 사람   결혼하다
her father was unwilling to give her to so fear-
꺼리는, 싫어하는   무시무시한
some a husband, and yet didn't want to offend
남편   불쾌하게 하다
the Lion; so he hit upon the following expedient.
…을 (우연히) 생각해내다   방편, 처방, 방책
He went to the Lion and said, "I think you
will make a very good husband for my daughter:
but I cannot consent to your union unless you
동의하다, 허락하다   연방, 연합
let me draw your teeth and pare your nails, for
뽑다   이빨   깎다   손톱·발톱
my daughter is terribly afraid of them."
몹시, 끔찍하게
The Lion was so much in love that he readily
사랑에 빠진   선뜻, 기꺼이
agreed that this should be done. When once,
동의하다, 합의하다
however, he was thus disarmed, the Cottager
무장을 해제하다, 무기를 빼앗다
was afraid of him no longer, but drove him away
쫓아내다, 추방하다
with his club.
곤봉, 방망이

216

THE BEE-KEEPER

A Thief found his way into an apiary when
도둑   발견하다, 알다   양봉장
the Bee-keeper was away, and stole all the
양봉가, 벌 기르는 사람   훔치다
honey. When the Keeper returned and found
꿀   돌아오다, 귀가하다
the hives empty, he was very much upset and
벌집   텅 빈   속상한, 마음이 상한
stood staring at them for some time.
응시하다, 노려보다

Before long the bees came back from gather-
(꿀)벌 돌아오다   모으기, 수집
ing honey, and, finding their hives overturned
뒤집다, 엎다, 넘어뜨리다
and the Keeper standing by, they made for him

with their stings.
침

At this he fell into a passion and cried, "You
벌컥 화를 내다, 노발대발하다
ungrateful scoundrels, you let the thief who
은혜를 모르는, 배은망덕한 악당, 나쁜놈
stole my honey get off scot-free, and then you go
완전히 자유롭게, 형벌 받지 않고
and sting me who have always taken such care
늘, 언제나   돌보다
of you!"

When you hit back make sure you have
반격하다, 되받아치다   확신
got the right man.
옳은, 정당한

217

THE WOLF AND THE HORSE

A Wolf on his rambles came to a field of
늑대   (전원 속을) 걷다[거닐다]   귀리 밭
oats, but, not being able to eat them, he

was passing on his way when a Horse came
지나가다, 통과하다   말
along.

"Look," said the Wolf, "here's a fine field
                                        훌륭한, 멋진
of oats. For your sake I have left it untouched,
        너를 위해서   남겨두다   손대지 않다, 건드리지 않다
and I shall greatly enjoy the sound of your teeth
                    즐거운, 기쁜
munching the ripe grain."
아삭아삭[우적우적] 먹다

But the Horse replied, "If wolves could eat

oats, my fine friend, you would hardly have

indulged your ears at the cost of your belly."
(욕구·관심 등을) 채우다[충족시키다]   배

> There is no virtue in giving to others what
>   미덕, 덕목
> is useless to oneself.
>   소용없는

THE WASP AND THE SNAKE

A Wasp settled on the head of a Snake, and
말벌   정착하다, 거주하다, 자리잡다   뱀
not only stung him several times, but
~뿐만 아니라   찌르다   여러 번, 몇 번
clung obstinately to the head of his victim.
꼭 붙잡다, 매달리다   고집 세게, 완강하게   피해자, 희생자

Maddened with pain the Snake tried every
…를 미치게[정말 화나게] 만들다(=infuriate)   모든
means he could think of to get rid of the crea-
수단, 방법   ~을 처리하다[없애다]
ture, but without success.
                성공

At last he became desperate, and crying,
                자포자기한, 필사적인
"Kill you I will, even at the cost of my own life,"
                ~조차, ~하더라도   비용이 들다, 대가를 치르다
he laid his head with the Wasp on it under
놓다, 두다(lay)   ~밑에
the wheel of a passing waggon, and they both
바퀴   지나가는   짐마차   둘 다
perished together.
(끔찍하게) 죽다, 비명횡사하다

THE FOWLER AND THE LARK

A Fowler was setting his nets for little birds
새 사냥꾼 / 설치하다 / 그물 / 작은 / 새
when a Lark came up to him and asked
종달새 / 다가오다, 가까이 오다
him what he was doing.

"I am engaged in founding a city," said he,
…으로 바쁘다, …에 종사하고 있다 / 건설하다 / 도시
and with that he withdrew to a short distance
물러나다, 철수하다(withdraw)
and concealed himself.
감추다, 숨기다
The Lark examined the nets with great
조사하다, 검토하다
curiosity, and presently, catching sight of the
호기심 / 곧, 이내 / 잡다 / 광경
bait, hopped on to them in order to secure it,
미끼 / ~하기 위해서 / 획득하다, 확보하다
and became entangled in the meshes.
얽어매다, (걸어서) 꼼짝 못하게 하다 / 그물망, 철망
The Fowler then ran up quickly and cap-
달려나오다 / 재빨리, 신속하게
tured her.

"What a fool I was!" said she: "but at any
바보, 멍청이 / 어쨌든, 하여튼
rate, if that's the kind of city you are founding,
종류 / 도시 / 건설하다
it'll be a long time before you find fools enough
~전에 / 발견하다, 찾아내다
to fill it."
(가득) 채우다[메우다]

THE FISHERMAN PIPING

A Fisherman who could play the flute went down one day to the sea-shore with his nets and his flute; and, taking his stand on a projecting rock, began to play a tune, thinking that the music would bring the fish jumping out of the sea.

He went on playing for some time, but not a fish appeared: so at last he threw down his flute and cast his net into the sea, and made a great haul of fish.

When they were landed and he saw them leaping about on the shore, he cried, "You rascals! you wouldn't dance when I piped: but now I've stopped, you can do nothing else!"

THE WEASEL AND THE MAN

A Man once caught a Weasel, which was al-
족제비
ways sneaking about the house, and was
살금살금[몰래] 가다(=creep)
just going to drown it in a tub of water, when it
딱, 꼭, 바로~   익사시키다   (뚜껑이 없고 둥글게 생긴 큰) 통
begged hard for its life, and said to him, "Surely
애원하다, 간청하다   확실히, 분명히
you haven't the heart to put me to death? Think
심장, 가슴; 마음
how useful I have been in clearing your house of
유용한, 도움이 되는, 쓸모 있는   청소, 깨끗이 치우기
the mice and lizards which used to infest it, and
쥐(mouse의 복수) 도마뱀   들끓다, 우글거리다
show your gratitude by sparing my life."
고마움, 감사   (상해, 죽음 등을) 피하게 해 주다
"You have not been altogether useless, I
완전히, 전적으로   소용없는, 쓸모 없는
grant you," said the Man: "but who killed the
(내키지 않지만) 인정하다
fowls? Who stole the meat? No, no! You do
가금   훔치다   고기
much more harm than good, and die you shall."
~보다 훨씬 더   해, 피해, 손해

THE PLOUGHMAN, THE ASS, AND THE OX

A Ploughman yoked his Ox and his Ass together, and set to work to plough his field. It was a poor makeshift of a team, but it was the best he could do, as he had but a single Ox. At the end of the day, when the beasts were loosed from the yoke, the Ass said to the Ox, "Well, we've had a hard day: which of us is to carry the master home?"

The Ox looked surprised at the question. "Why," said he, "you, to be sure, as usual."

DEMADES AND HIS FABLE

Demades the orator was once speaking in
데마데스   연설가, 웅변가
the Assembly at Athens; but the people
의회, 입법 기관
were very inattentive to what he was saying, so
주의를 기울이지 않는, 신경을 쓰지 않는
he stopped and said, "Gentlemen, I should like
to tell you one of Aesop's fables."
우화; 설화, 이야기
This made every one listen intently.
강한 관심을 갖고, 골똘하게
Then Demades began: "Demeter, a Swallow,
데메테르(농업의 여신) 제비
and an Eel were once travelling together, and
뱀장어   (장거리) 여행을 하다
came to a river without a bridge: the Swallow
강   다리
flew over it, and the Eel swam across"; and then
날아서 건너다   건너서, 가로질러
he stopped.
멈추다, 중단하다
"What happened to Demeter?" cried several
(어떤 일이) ~에게 일어나다[생기다], ~이 …게 되다
people in the audience.
청중, 관중
"Demeter," he replied, "is very angry with
대답하다   화난, 성난
you for listening to fables when you ought to be
…해야 하다
minding public business."
대중을 위한, 공공의

THE CROW AND THE SNAKE

A hungry Crow spied a Snake lying asleep in a sunny spot, and, picking it up in his claws, he was carrying it off to a place where he could make a meal of it without being disturbed, when the Snake reared its head and bit him. It was a poisonous Snake, and the bite was fatal, and the dying Crow said, "What a cruel fate is mine! I thought I had made a lucky find, and it has cost me my life!"

THE MONKEY AND THE DOLPHIN

When people go on a voyage they often take with them lap-dogs or monkeys as pets to wile away the time. Thus it fell out that a man returning to Athens from the East had a pet Monkey on board with him.

As they neared the coast of Attica a great storm burst upon them, and the ship capsized. All on board were thrown into the water, and tried to save themselves by swimming, the Monkey among the rest.

A Dolphin saw him, and, supposing him to be a man, took him on his back and began swimming towards the shore.

When they got near the Piraeus, which is the
port of Athens, the Dolphin asked the Monkey
if he was an Athenian. The Monkey replied that
he was, and added that he came of a very distin-
guished family.

"Then, of course, you know the Piraeus,"
continued the Dolphin. The Monkey thought he
was referring to some high official or other, and
replied, "Oh, yes, he's a very old friend of mine."
At that, detecting his hypocrisy, the Dolphin
was so disgusted that he dived below the surface, and the unfortunate Monkey was quickly
drowned.

THE NIGHTINGALE AND THE HAWK

A Nightingale was sitting on a bough of an
나이팅게일, 꾀꼬리   (나무의 큰) 가지
oak and singing, as her custom was.
오크 나무, 떡갈나무   습관(=habit, practice)
A hungry Hawk presently spied her, and
매   곧, 이내   엿보다, 염탐하다
darting to the spot seized her in his talons.
쏜살같이[휙] 달리다[움직이다]   꽉 붙잡다   (맹금류의 갈고리 모양) 발톱
He was just about to tear her in pieces when
막 ~하려고 하다   찢다   산산조각으로
she begged him to spare her life: "I'm not big
큰
enough," she pleaded, "to make you a good
충분히   애원하다 (=beg)
meal: you ought to seek your prey among the
식사, 끼니   찾다, 구하다, 추구하다   먹이
bigger birds."
더 큰
The Hawk eyed her with some contempt.
경멸, 멸시
"You must think me very simple," said he, "if
단순한, 머리가 둔한
you suppose I am going to give up a certain
~라고 여기다[생각하다, 추정하다]   포기하다   확실한, 분명한
prize on the chance of a better of which I see at
상(품)   기회   더 나은
present no signs."
현재, 지금   기미, 조짐

THE ROSE AND THE AMARANTH

A Rose and an Amaranth blossomed side by side in a garden, and the Amaranth said to her neighbour, "How I envy you your beauty and your sweet scent! No wonder you are such a universal favourite."

But the Rose replied with a shade of sadness in her voice, "Ah, my dear friend, I bloom but for a time: my petals soon wither and fall, and then I die. But your flowers never fade, even if they are cut; for they are everlasting."

장미 / 아마란스 / 꽃이 피다, 꽃을 피우다 / 나란히 / 정원, 뜰 / 이웃(사람) / 부러워하다, 선망하다 / 아름다움 / 달콤한 / 향기 / 놀라운, 경이로운 / 일반적인, 전 세계적인 / 좋아하는 사람[것] / 대꾸하다 / 그늘 / 슬픔 / 꽃이 피다(=flower) / 꽃잎 / 시들다, 말라 죽다 / 색이 바래다, 시들해지다 / 영원한, 변치 않는

THE MAN, THE HORSE, THE OX, AND THE DOG

One winter's day, during a severe storm, a Horse, an Ox, and a Dog came and begged for shelter in the house of a Man.

He readily admitted them, and, as they were cold and wet, he lit a fire for their comfort: and he put oats before the Horse, and hay before the Ox, while he fed the Dog with the remains of his own dinner.

When the storm abated, and they were about to depart, they determined to show their gratitude in the following way.

They divided the life of Man among them, and each endowed one part of it with the qualities which were peculiarly his own.

232

The Horse took youth, and hence young men
are high-mettled and impatient of restraint; the
Ox took middle age, and accordingly men in
middle life are steady and hard-working; while
the Dog took old age, which is the reason why
old men are so often peevish and ill-tempered,
and, like dogs, attached chiefly to those who
look to their comfort, while they are disposed to
snap at those who are unfamiliar or distasteful
to them.

THE WOLF AND HIS SHADOW

A Wolf, who was roaming about on the plain
늑대 (이리저리) 돌아다니다, 배회[방랑]하다(=wander)
when the sun was getting low in the sky,
해, 태양 낮은
was much impressed by the size of his shadow,
감명[감동]을 주다 크기 그림자
and said to himself, "I had no idea I was so big.
~를 전혀 몰랐다
Fancy my being afraid of a lion! Why, I, not he,
상상, 공상
ought to be King of the beasts"; and, heedless of
마땅히 ~해야 하다 왕 짐승, 야수 위험에 부주의한
danger, he strutted about as if there could be no
뽐내며[거들먹거리며] 걷다 의심
doubt at all about it.
할 여지 없이

Just then a lion sprang upon him and began
바로 그때 (갑자기) 뛰어오르다(spring)
to devour him.
집어삼킬듯이[빨아들이듯이] 보다

"Alas," he cried, "had I not lost sight of the
외치다 시력을 잃다
facts, I shouldn't have been ruined by my fan-
사실, 현실, 실제 파멸하다
cies."

MERCURY AND THE MAN BITTEN BY AN ANT

A Man once saw (보다) a ship (배) go down (가라앉다, 침몰하다) with all its crew (승무원, 선원), and commented (논평하다, 견해를 밝히다) severely (신랄하게, 혹독하게) on the injustice (불평등; 부당함, 부당성) of the gods.

"They care nothing (…에 관심이 없다, 전혀 신경 쓰지 않다) for a man's character (성격, 기질, 개성)," said he, "but let (~하게 하다) the good and the bad go to their deaths (죽음) together."

There was an ant-heap (개미집) close by (~가까이, ~근처에) where he was standing, and, just as he spoke (말하다(speak)), he was bitten in the foot (발) by an Ant (개미).

Turning in a temper (울화통, 분통, 성남) to the ant-heap he stamped (짓밟다, 마구 밟다) upon it and crushed (으스러[쭈그러]뜨리다) hundreds of unoffending (죄가 없는, 무고한) ants.

Suddenly (갑자기, 불현듯) Mercury (메르쿠리우스(상업의 신)의 영어 이름) appeared, and belaboured (세게 치다, 때리다) him with his staff (지팡이), saying as he did so, "You villain (악당, 악한), where's your nice (멋진, 훌륭한) sense of justice (정의감) now?"

THE STAG AND THE LION

A Stag was chased by the hounds, and took
수사슴   쫓다, 추격하다   사냥개
refuge in a cave, where he hoped to be safe
피난(처), 피신(처), 도피(처)   바라다, 희망하다   안전한
from his pursuers.
뒤쫓는 사람, 추적[격]자

Unfortunately the cave contained a Lion, to
재수없게, 불운하게, 운 나쁘게   동굴   …이 들어[함유되어] 있다
whom he fell an easy prey.
쉬운   먹이

"Unhappy that I am," he cried, "I am saved
불행한, 재수 없는   구하다
from the power of the dogs only to fall into the
힘, 세력
clutches of a Lion."
손아귀, 마수

Out of the frying-pan into the fire.
~밖으로 나오다   프라이팬   불

237

THE LION, THE FOX, AND THE ASS

A Lion, a Fox, and an Ass went out hunting together. They had soon taken a large booty, which the Lion requested the Ass to divide between them.

The Ass divided it all into three equal parts, and modestly begged the others to take their choice; at which the Lion, bursting with fury, sprang upon the Ass and tore him to pieces.

Then, glaring at the Fox, he bade him make a fresh division. The Fox gathered almost the whole in one great heap for the Lion's share, leaving only the smallest possible morsel for himself.

"My dear friend," said the Lion, "how did you get the knack of it so well?"

The Fox replied, "Me? Oh, I took a lesson from the Ass."

Happy is he who learns from the misfor-
행복   ~로부터 배우다   불운, 불행
tunes of others.
         다른 사람

THE EAGLE AND THE FOX

An Eagle and a Fox became great friends
독수리   여우   ~가 되다
and determined to live near one an-
결심하다, 결정하다   가까이에서
other: they thought that the more they saw of
보다
each other the better friends they would be.
서로   더 나은, 더 좋은
So the Eagle built a nest at the top of a high
둥지를 틀다   꼭대기   높은
tree, while the Fox settled in a thicket at the foot
정착하다, 거주하다 덤불, 잡목 숲   밑동
of it and produced a litter of cubs.
낳다, 생산하다   한배에서난 ~의 새끼
One day the Fox went out foraging for food,
먹이를 찾다
and the Eagle, who also wanted food for her
~도, 역시   음식, 먹이
young, flew down into the thicket, caught up the
새끼   날아 내려오다   덤불, 잡목 숲 잡아가다
Fox's cubs, and carried them up into the tree for
새끼   나르다, 운반하다
a meal for herself and her family.
식사, 끼니   가족
When the Fox came back, and found out
돌아오다   …임을 알아내다, 발견하다
what had happened, she was not so much sorry
(~일이) 있다[발생하다/벌어지다]
for the loss of her cubs as furious because she
분실, 상실   몹시 화가 난, 격분한
couldn't get at the Eagle and pay her out for her
treachery.
배반, 배신
So she sat down not far off and cursed her.
멀리 떨어진   저주하다
But it wasn't long before she had her revenge.
복수

Some villagers happened to be sacrificing a
goat on a neighbouring altar, and the Eagle flew
down and carried off a piece of burning flesh to
her nest.

There was a strong wind blowing, and the
nest caught fire, with the result that her fledg-
lings fell half-roasted to the ground.

Then the Fox ran to the spot and devoured
them in full sight of the Eagle.

False faith may escape human punishment, but cannot escape the divine.

THE GNAT AND THE LION

A Gnat once went up to a Lion and said, "I
am not in the least afraid of you: I don't
even allow that you are a match for me in
strength. What does your strength amount to
after all? That you can scratch with your claws
and bite with your teeth--just like a woman in
a temper--and nothing more. But I'm stronger
than you: if you don't believe it, let us fight and
see."

So saying, the Gnat sounded his horn, and
소리내다　　　　　뿔피리
darted in and bit the Lion on the nose. When the
쏜살같이 날아들다　깨물다　　　　　코
Lion felt the sting, in his haste to crush him he
느끼다　　침　　　서두름, 급함(=hurry)
scratched his nose badly, and made it bleed, but
긁다　　　　심하게, 세게　　　　　출혈하다, 피가 나다
failed altogether to hurt the Gnat, which buzzed
실패하다　완전히, 전적으로　다치게 하다, 상처를 주다　　윙윙거리다
off in triumph, elated by its victory. Presently,
대승을 거두어, 의기 양양하여　　　승리　　　이내, 곧
however, it got entangled in a spider's web, and
하지만, 어쨌든　　　얽어매다, (걸어서) 꼼짝 못하게 하다　거미의 그물
was caught and eaten by the spider, thus falling
거미
a prey to an insignificant insect after having tri-
먹이　　　　하찮은, 보잘것없는　　곤충
umphed over the King of the Beasts.

HERCULES AND MINERVA

Hercules was once travelling along a narrow
헤라클레스(제우스 신의 아들로 힘센 영웅)   …을 (계속) 따라   좁은
road when he saw lying on the ground in
도로, 길   놓여 있는, 놓인   땅바닥, 지면
front of him what appeared to be an apple, and
~앞쪽에   …인 것 같다(=seem)   사과
as he passed he stamped upon it with his heel.
         지나가다, 통과하다   발로 밟다   뒤꿈치
To his astonishment, instead of being
         깜짝[크게] 놀람(=amazement)   ~대신에
crushed it doubled in size; and, on his attacking
으스러[쭈그러]뜨리다; 바수다   크기   공격
it again and smiting it with his club, it swelled
     다시   세게 치다[때리다], 공격하다   곤봉, 방망이   부풀다, 부어오르다
up to an enormous size and blocked up the
         막대한, 거대한(=huge, immense)   (지나가지 못하게) 막다, 차단하다
whole road.

Upon this he dropped his club, and stood
                        떨어뜨리다
looking at it in amazement.
~을 쳐다보다[바라보다]   깜짝 놀람, 크게 놀람
Just then Minerva appeared, and said to
                    미네르바(그리스 신화의 아테나)
him, "Leave it alone, my friend; that which you
         그냥 내버려두다, 방치하다
see before you is the apple of discord: if you do
                                    불화, 다툼
not meddle with it, it remains small as it was at
         간섭하다, 참견하다, 끼어들다   작은, 적은
first, but if you resort to violence it swells into
                    호소하다   폭력, 폭행; 난폭(한 조치)
the thing you see."

THE FOX AND THE LEOPARD

A Fox and a Leopard were disputing about
여우   표범   논쟁하다; (…에 대하여) 말다툼하다
their looks, and each claimed to be the
          외모, 용모, 모습   ~라고 주장하다
more handsome of the two.
멋진, 잘생긴

The Leopard said, "Look at my smart coat;
                    단정한, 말쑥한, 멋진
you have nothing to match that."
                    …에 필적하다

But the Fox replied, "Your coat may be

smart, but my wits are smarter still."
          재치, 지혜, 꾀, 슬기

THE CROW AND THE RAVEN

A Crow became very jealous of a Raven, because the latter was regarded by men as a
bird of omen which foretold the future, and was
accordingly held in great respect by them.
She was very anxious to get the same sort of
reputation herself; and, one day, seeing some
travellers approaching, she flew on to a branch
of a tree at the roadside and cawed as loud as
she could.

The travellers were in some dismay at the
sound, for they feared it might be a bad omen;
till one of them, spying the Crow, said to his
companions, "It's all right, my friends, we can
go on without fear, for it's only a crow and that
means nothing."

Those who pretend to be something they
are not only make themselves ridiculous.

THE WITCH

A Witch professed to be able to avert the
마녀, 여자마법사   공언하다, 단언하다   막다, 피하다
anger of the gods by means of charms, of
노여움, 화, 분노, 격노   마력, 마법, 부적, 주문
which she alone possessed the secret; and she
                소유하다, 가지다, 갖고 있다   비밀, 비결
drove a brisk trade, and made a fat livelihood
장사[사업]가 번성[번창]하다   생계(의 수단), 살림
out of it.

But certain persons accused her of black
      어느, 어떤   고소하다   흑마법
magic and carried her before the judges, and
            데려가다, 끌고가다   심판, 판사, 판관
demanded that she should be put to death for
…을 요구[청구]하다; …을 [남에게] 강력히 요구하다   죽음
dealings with the Devil.
거래   악마
She was found guilty and condemned to
            유죄의, […의] 책임이 있는   (…형을) 선고하다
death: and one of the judges said to her as she

was leaving the dock, "You say you can avert the
            (형사법정의) 피고석   막다, 피하다
anger of the gods. How comes it, then, that you
                      어떻게, 왜
have failed to disarm the enmity of men?"
    실패하다   무장을 해제하다   증오, 원한, 적의

THE MISER

A Miser sold everything he had, and melted down his hoard of gold into a single lump, which he buried secretly in a field.

Every day he went to look at it, and would sometimes spend long hours gloating over his treasure.

One of his men noticed his frequent visits to the spot, and one day watched him and discovered his secret.

Waiting his opportunity, he went one night and dug up the gold and stole it.

Next day the Miser visited the place as usual, and, finding his treasure gone, fell to tearing his hair and groaning over his loss.

In this condition he was seen by one of his neighbours, who asked him what his trouble was.

The Miser told him of his misfortune; but
_{불운, 불행}
the other replied, "Don't take it so much to
_{다른 사람}   _{대답하다, 응대하다}
heart, my friend; put a brick into the hole, and
_{벽돌}   _{구멍}
take a look at it every day: you won't be any

worse off than before, for even when you had
_{악화되어 있는, 더 나쁜}
your gold it was of no earthly use to you."
_{전혀 쓸모 없는}

249

THE HUNTER AND THE WOODMAN

A Hunter was searching in the forest for the
사냥꾼   찾다, 조사하다, 뒤지다, 수색하다
tracks of a lion, and, catching sight pres-
(사람, 짐승이 지나간) 자국   광경, 풍경, 전망
ently of a Woodman engaged in felling a tree, he
나무꾼, 벌목꾼   ~하느라 바쁜
went up to him and asked him if he had noticed
다가가다, 가까이 가다   보다, 주목하다
a lion's footprints anywhere about, or if he knew
발자국   어디(로)든지
where his den was.
동굴

The Woodman answered, "If you will come
대답하다
with me, I will show you the lion himself."
보여주다

The Hunter turned pale with fear, and his
창백해지다   공포, 두려움
teeth chattered as he replied, "Oh, I'm not look-
[공포로] 딱딱 맞부딪치다   ~을 찾다
ing for the lion, thanks, but only for his tracks."
그저, 단지   흔적, 발자국

THE SERPENT AND THE EAGLE

An Eagle swooped down upon a Serpent
독수리　　갑자기 덮치다, 급습하다　　　　　뱀
and seized it in his talons with the
꽉 붙잡다[움켜쥐다]　　[맹금의] 발톱
intention of carrying it off and devouring it. But
의도, 의향, 의지　　　　　　　　　　　　먹어치우다, 잡아먹다
the Serpent was too quick for him and had its
빠른
coils round him in a moment; and then there
돌돌 감다, 칭칭 감다　　　순식간에
ensued a life-and-death struggle between the
계속되다, 잇따라 일어나다　　　　결투, 투쟁, 싸움
two.

A countryman, who was a witness of the
시골 사람, 촌사람; 농민　　　　목격자
encounter, came to the assistance of the Eagle,
충돌, 싸움　　　　　　　도움, 원조, 지원, 보조
and succeeded in freeing him from the Serpent
성공하다　　　　자유로운; 해방시키다
and enabling him to escape.
… 할 수 있게 하다　　도망치다, 달아나다
In revenge the Serpent spat some of his
침을 뱉다
poison into the man's drinking-horn. Heated
독　　　　　　　　뿔(로 만든) 잔　　열이 나다, 더워지다
with his exertions, the man was about to slake
노력, 진력; 고된[어려운] 일　　　　　　…을 축이다
his thirst with a draught from the horn, when
갈증　　　　　(물, 술 등을) 통에서 따르기
the Eagle knocked it out of his hand, and spilled
~에 부딪쳐 제거하다　　　　　　　　엎지르다, 쏟다
its contents upon the ground.
들어 있는, 함유하고 있는

One good turn deserves another.
선(행)　　　　　[…을] 받을 만하다, …의 가치가 있다

THE DOG CHASING A WOLF

A Dog was chasing a Wolf, and as he ran he
뒤쫓다, 추격하다   늑대   달리다
thought what a fine fellow he was, and
       멋진, 훌륭한
what strong legs he had, and how quickly they
      강한, 튼튼한   다리   재빨리, 빠르게
covered the ground.
(~을) 여행하다, 가다, 답파하다
  "Now, there's this Wolf," he said to himself,
"what a poor creature he is: he's no match for
      가련한, 불쌍한   (~의) 적수가 되다
me, and he knows it and so he runs away."
        알다   도망치다, 달아나다
  But the Wolf looked round just then and
             돌아보다
said, "Don't you imagine I'm running away from
              (~라고) 생각하다, 상상하다
you, my friend: it's your master I'm afraid of."
                           주인   ~을 두려워하다

THE HAWK, THE KITE, AND THE PIGEONS

The Pigeons in a certain dovecote were
비둘기   비둘기장
persecuted by a Kite, who every now and
박해하다, 고통받다   솔개   모든, ~마다 때때로, 이따금
then swooped down and carried off one of their
급습하다, 급강하하다   채가다
number.

So they invited a Hawk into the dovecote to
초대하다   매   비둘기장
defend them against their enemy.
…을 방어[방위]하다, 지키다, 막다   적
But they soon repented of their folly: for the
후회하다, 유감으로 여기다   어리석음, 바보짓
Hawk killed more of them in a day than the Kite
죽이다   하루에
had done in a year.
1년에

THE HORSE AND THE ASS

A Horse, proud of his fine harness, met an
말 ~을 자랑스러워하다   (마차 말의) 마구
Ass on the high-road. As the Ass with his
나귀   잔뜩 높이 쌓아 실은 짐
heavy burden moved slowly out of the way to let
무거운   짐   움직이다   느리게, 천천히
him pass, the Horse cried out impatiently that
지나가다, 통과하다   고함을 지르다   참지 못하고, 성급하게
he could hardly resist kicking him to make him
참다, 견디다
move faster.
더 빨리

The Ass held his peace, but did not forget the
잠자코 있다, 아무 말 하지 않다   잊다, 잊어버리다
other's insolence.
오만[무례]한 태도[말]

Not long afterwards the Horse became
~뒤에, ~다음에
broken-winded, and was sold by his owner to a
숨이 찬; [말이] 폐기종의   팔다   소유주, 주인
farmer.
농부

One day, as he was drawing a dung-cart, he
거름 운반차, 두엄차
met the Ass again, who in turn derided him and
조소하다, …을 비웃다
said, "Aha! you never thought to come to this,
절대로, 결코
did you, you who were so proud! Where are all
your gay trappings now?"
화려한 말의 장식

PROMETHEUS AND THE MAKING OF MAN

At the bidding of Jupiter, Prometheus
명령, 지시　　　　　　　프로메테우스(그리스신화)
set about the creation of Man and the
창조; 창시, 창설
other animals.
동물
Jupiter, seeing that Mankind, the only
인류, 인간
rational creatures, were far outnumbered by the
이성적인, 분별 있는, 양식 있는　　　　　　…보다 수가 많다
irrational beasts, bade him redress the balance
비이성적인, 분별 없는　　명령하다(bid)　다시 손질하다, 바로잡다　균형
by turning some of the latter into men.
후자
Prometheus did as he was bidden, and this is
~대로
the reason why some people have the forms of
이유, 까닭, 근거　　　　　　　　　　　형태, 모습, 모양
men but the souls of beasts.
영혼; 정신, 마음

THE HUNTER AND THE HORSEMAN

A Hunter went out after game, and succeeded in catching a hare, which he was carrying home with him when he met a man on horseback, who said to him, "You have had some sport I see, sir," and offered to buy it.

The Hunter readily agreed; but the Horseman had no sooner got the hare in his hands than he set spurs to his horse and went off at full gallop.

The Hunter ran after him for some little distance; but it soon dawned upon him that he had been tricked, and he gave up trying to overtake the Horseman, and, to save his face, called after him as loud as he could, "All right, sir, all right, take your hare: it was meant all along as a present."

THE NIGHTINGALE AND THE SWALLOW

A Swallow, conversing with a Nightingale,
제비 대화를 나누다 나이팅게일, 꾀꼬리
advised her to quit the leafy coverts where
조언하다, 충고하다 그만두다, 떠나다 잎으로 덮인
she made her home, and to come and live with

men, like herself, and nest under the shelter of
인간, 사람 둥지를 틀다 피난처, 피신처
their roofs.
지붕
But the Nightingale replied, "Time was when

I too, like yourself, lived among men: but the
~처럼 ~사이에서
memory of the cruel wrongs I then suffered
기억, 추억 잔인한, 모진, 무자비한 고통을 받다
makes them hateful to me, and never again will
몹시 싫은, 지긋지긋한
I approach their dwellings."
가까이 다가가다, 접근하다 거처, 거주지, 주택

The scene of past sufferings revives pain-
장면, 현장 과거 소생시키다, 되살아나게 하다
ful memories.
기억

THE TRAVELLER AND FORTUNE

A Traveller, exhausted with fatigue after a long journey, sank down at the very brink of a deep well and presently fell asleep. He was within an ace of falling in, when Dame Fortune appeared to him and touched him on the shoulder, cautioning him to move further away.

"Wake up, good sir, I pray you," she said; "had you fallen into the well, the blame would have been thrown not on your own folly but on me, Fortune."

여행자, 여행객 · 지치다, 녹초가 되다 · 피로, 피곤 · 장거리 여행 · 가라앉다[빠지다](sink) · 가장자리, 언저리, 끝 · 깊은 우물 · 곧, 이내 · 잠들다 · 막 …할 찰나에 · 떨어짐, 낙하 · 행운의 여신 · 나타나다, 모습을 드러내다 · 만지다, 손을 대다 · 어깨 · (…에 대하여) 경고[주의]를 주다, 조심시키다 · 비난, 책망; 책임 · 던지다 · 어리석음, 우둔함

📖 나만의 리뷰 and 명문장

📚 나만의 리뷰 and 명문장